C-204 CAREER EXAMINATION SERIES

This is your
PASSBOOK for...

Deputy Sheriff

Test Preparation Study Guide
Questions & Answers

NATIONAL LEARNING CORPORATION®

COPYRIGHT NOTICE

This book is SOLELY intended for, is sold ONLY to, and its use is RESTRICTED to individual, bona fide applicants or candidates who qualify by virtue of having seriously filed applications for appropriate license, certificate, professional and/or promotional advancement, higher school matriculation, scholarship, or other legitimate requirements of education and/or governmental authorities.

This book is NOT intended for use, class instruction, tutoring, training, duplication, copying, reprinting, excerption, or adaptation, etc., by:

1) Other publishers
2) Proprietors and/or Instructors of "Coaching" and/or Preparatory Courses
3) Personnel and/or Training Divisions of commercial, industrial, and governmental organizations
4) Schools, colleges, or universities and/or their departments and staffs, including teachers and other personnel
5) Testing Agencies or Bureaus
6) Study groups which seek by the purchase of a single volume to copy and/or duplicate and/or adapt this material for use by the group as a whole without having purchased individual volumes for each of the members of the group
7) Et al.

Such persons would be in violation of appropriate Federal and State statutes.

PROVISION OF LICENSING AGREEMENTS – Recognized educational, commercial, industrial, and governmental institutions and organizations, and others legitimately engaged in educational pursuits, including training, testing, and measurement activities, may address request for a licensing agreement to the copyright owners, who will determine whether, and under what conditions, including fees and charges, the materials in this book may be used them. In other words, a licensing facility exists for the legitimate use of the material in this book on other than an individual basis. However, it is asseverated and affirmed here that the material in this book CANNOT be used without the receipt of the express permission of such a licensing agreement from the Publishers. Inquiries re licensing should be addressed to the company, attention rights and permissions department.

All rights reserved, including the right of reproduction in whole or in part, in any form or by any means, electronic or mechanical, including photocopying, recording, or by any information storage and retrieval system, without permission in writing from the Publisher.

Copyright © 2024 by
National Learning Corporation

212 Michael Drive, Syosset, NY 11791
(516) 921-8888 • www.passbooks.com
E-mail: info@passbooks.com

PUBLISHED IN THE UNITED STATES OF AMERICA

PASSBOOK® SERIES

THE *PASSBOOK® SERIES* has been created to prepare applicants and candidates for the ultimate academic battlefield – the examination room.

At some time in our lives, each and every one of us may be required to take an examination – for validation, matriculation, admission, qualification, registration, certification, or licensure.

Based on the assumption that every applicant or candidate has met the basic formal educational standards, has taken the required number of courses, and read the necessary texts, the *PASSBOOK® SERIES* furnishes the one special preparation which may assure passing with confidence, instead of failing with insecurity. Examination questions – together with answers – are furnished as the basic vehicle for study so that the mysteries of the examination and its compounding difficulties may be eliminated or diminished by a sure method.

This book is meant to help you pass your examination provided that you qualify and are serious in your objective.

The entire field is reviewed through the huge store of content information which is succinctly presented through a provocative and challenging approach – the question-and-answer method.

A climate of success is established by furnishing the correct answers at the end of each test.

You soon learn to recognize types of questions, forms of questions, and patterns of questioning. You may even begin to anticipate expected outcomes.

You perceive that many questions are repeated or adapted so that you can gain acute insights, which may enable you to score many sure points.

You learn how to confront new questions, or types of questions, and to attack them confidently and work out the correct answers.

You note objectives and emphases, and recognize pitfalls and dangers, so that you may make positive educational adjustments.

Moreover, you are kept fully informed in relation to new concepts, methods, practices, and directions in the field.

You discover that you are actually taking the examination all the time: you are preparing for the examination by "taking" an examination, not by reading extraneous and/or supererogatory textbooks.

In short, this PASSBOOK®, used directedly, should be an important factor in helping you to pass your test.

DEPUTY SHERIFF

DUTIES:
Performs specific law enforcement and security duties particular to the Department of the Sheriff, transports inmates and detainees, and executes warrants and court orders; performs related duties as required.

SCOPE OF THE EXAMINATION:
The written test will be designed to test for knowledge, skills, and/or abilities in such areas as:
1. **Applying written information (laws, rules, regulations, procedures, etc.) in civil law enforcement and court-related situations** - These questions test how well you can apply written information, in the form of rules, to given situations similar to those typically encountered by civil law enforcement employees, court attendants, and court security officers. All information needed to answer the questions is contained in the rules, regulations, etc., which are cited.
2. **Following directions (maps)** - These questions test your ability to follow physical/geographic directions using street maps or building maps. You will have to read and understand a set of directions and then use them on a simple map.
3. **Preparing written material** - These questions test for the ability to present information clearly and accurately, and to organize paragraphs logically and comprehensibly. For some questions, you will be given information in two or three sentences followed by four restatements of the information. You must then choose the best version. For other questions, you will be given paragraphs with their sentences out of order. You must then choose, from four suggestions, the best order for the sentences.
4. **Public contact principles and practices** - These questions test for knowledge of techniques used to interact with other people, to gather and present information, and to provide assistance, advice, and effective customer service in a courteous and professional manner. Questions will cover such topics as understanding and responding to people with diverse needs, perspectives, personalities, and levels of familiarity with agency operations, as well as acting in a way that both serves the public and reflects well on your agency.

HOW TO TAKE A TEST

I. YOU MUST PASS AN EXAMINATION

A. *WHAT EVERY CANDIDATE SHOULD KNOW*

Examination applicants often ask us for help in preparing for the written test. What can I study in advance? What kinds of questions will be asked? How will the test be given? How will the papers be graded?

As an applicant for a civil service examination, you may be wondering about some of these things. Our purpose here is to suggest effective methods of advance study and to describe civil service examinations.

Your chances for success on this examination can be increased if you know how to prepare. Those "pre-examination jitters" can be reduced if you know what to expect. You can even experience an adventure in good citizenship if you know why civil service exams are given.

B. *WHY ARE CIVIL SERVICE EXAMINATIONS GIVEN?*

Civil service examinations are important to you in two ways. As a citizen, you want public jobs filled by employees who know how to do their work. As a job seeker, you want a fair chance to compete for that job on an equal footing with other candidates. The best-known means of accomplishing this two-fold goal is the competitive examination.

Exams are widely publicized throughout the nation. They may be administered for jobs in federal, state, city, municipal, town or village governments or agencies.

Any citizen may apply, with some limitations, such as the age or residence of applicants. Your experience and education may be reviewed to see whether you meet the requirements for the particular examination. When these requirements exist, they are reasonable and applied consistently to all applicants. Thus, a competitive examination may cause you some uneasiness now, but it is your privilege and safeguard.

C. *HOW ARE CIVIL SERVICE EXAMS DEVELOPED?*

Examinations are carefully written by trained technicians who are specialists in the field known as "psychological measurement," in consultation with recognized authorities in the field of work that the test will cover. These experts recommend the subject matter areas or skills to be tested; only those knowledges or skills important to your success on the job are included. The most reliable books and source materials available are used as references. Together, the experts and technicians judge the difficulty level of the questions.

Test technicians know how to phrase questions so that the problem is clearly stated. Their ethics do not permit "trick" or "catch" questions. Questions may have been tried out on sample groups, or subjected to statistical analysis, to determine their usefulness.

Written tests are often used in combination with performance tests, ratings of training and experience, and oral interviews. All of these measures combine to form the best-known means of finding the right person for the right job.

II. HOW TO PASS THE WRITTEN TEST

A. NATURE OF THE EXAMINATION

To prepare intelligently for civil service examinations, you should know how they differ from school examinations you have taken. In school you were assigned certain definite pages to read or subjects to cover. The examination questions were quite detailed and usually emphasized memory. Civil service exams, on the other hand, try to discover your present ability to perform the duties of a position, plus your potentiality to learn these duties. In other words, a civil service exam attempts to predict how successful you will be. Questions cover such a broad area that they cannot be as minute and detailed as school exam questions.

In the public service similar kinds of work, or positions, are grouped together in one "class." This process is known as *position-classification*. All the positions in a class are paid according to the salary range for that class. One class title covers all of these positions, and they are all tested by the same examination.

B. FOUR BASIC STEPS

1) Study the announcement

How, then, can you know what subjects to study? Our best answer is: "Learn as much as possible about the class of positions for which you've applied." The exam will test the knowledge, skills and abilities needed to do the work.

Your most valuable source of information about the position you want is the official exam announcement. This announcement lists the training and experience qualifications. Check these standards and apply only if you come reasonably close to meeting them.

The brief description of the position in the examination announcement offers some clues to the subjects which will be tested. Think about the job itself. Review the duties in your mind. Can you perform them, or are there some in which you are rusty? Fill in the blank spots in your preparation.

Many jurisdictions preview the written test in the exam announcement by including a section called "Knowledge and Abilities Required," "Scope of the Examination," or some similar heading. Here you will find out specifically what fields will be tested.

2) Review your own background

Once you learn in general what the position is all about, and what you need to know to do the work, ask yourself which subjects you already know fairly well and which need improvement. You may wonder whether to concentrate on improving your strong areas or on building some background in your fields of weakness. When the announcement has specified "some knowledge" or "considerable knowledge," or has used adjectives like "beginning principles of…" or "advanced … methods," you can get a clue as to the number and difficulty of questions to be asked in any given field. More questions, and hence broader coverage, would be included for those subjects which are more important in the work. Now weigh your strengths and weaknesses against the job requirements and prepare accordingly.

3) Determine the level of the position

Another way to tell how intensively you should prepare is to understand the level of the job for which you are applying. Is it the entering level? In other words, is this the position in which beginners in a field of work are hired? Or is it an intermediate or advanced level? Sometimes this is indicated by such words as "Junior" or "Senior" in the class title. Other jurisdictions use Roman numerals to designate the level – Clerk I, Clerk II, for example. The word "Supervisor" sometimes appears in the title. If the level is not indicated by the title, check the description of duties. Will you be working under very close supervision, or will you have responsibility for independent decisions in this work?

4) Choose appropriate study materials

Now that you know the subjects to be examined and the relative amount of each subject to be covered, you can choose suitable study materials. For beginning level jobs, or even advanced ones, if you have a pronounced weakness in some aspect of your training, read a modern, standard textbook in that field. Be sure it is up to date and has general coverage. Such books are normally available at your library, and the librarian will be glad to help you locate one. For entry-level positions, questions of appropriate difficulty are chosen – neither highly advanced questions, nor those too simple. Such questions require careful thought but not advanced training.

If the position for which you are applying is technical or advanced, you will read more advanced, specialized material. If you are already familiar with the basic principles of your field, elementary textbooks would waste your time. Concentrate on advanced textbooks and technical periodicals. Think through the concepts and review difficult problems in your field.

These are all general sources. You can get more ideas on your own initiative, following these leads. For example, training manuals and publications of the government agency which employs workers in your field can be useful, particularly for technical and professional positions. A letter or visit to the government department involved may result in more specific study suggestions, and certainly will provide you with a more definite idea of the exact nature of the position you are seeking.

III. KINDS OF TESTS

Tests are used for purposes other than measuring knowledge and ability to perform specified duties. For some positions, it is equally important to test ability to make adjustments to new situations or to profit from training. In others, basic mental abilities not dependent on information are essential. Questions which test these things may not appear as pertinent to the duties of the position as those which test for knowledge and information. Yet they are often highly important parts of a fair examination. For very general questions, it is almost impossible to help you direct your study efforts. What we can do is to point out some of the more common of these general abilities needed in public service positions and describe some typical questions.

1) General information

Broad, general information has been found useful for predicting job success in some kinds of work. This is tested in a variety of ways, from vocabulary lists to questions about current events. Basic background in some field of work, such as sociology or economics, may be sampled in a group of questions. Often these are principles which have become familiar to most persons through exposure rather than through formal training. It is difficult to advise you how to study for these questions; being alert to the world around you is our best suggestion.

2) Verbal ability

An example of an ability needed in many positions is verbal or language ability. Verbal ability is, in brief, the ability to use and understand words. Vocabulary and grammar tests are typical measures of this ability. Reading comprehension or paragraph interpretation questions are common in many kinds of civil service tests. You are given a paragraph of written material and asked to find its central meaning.

3) Numerical ability
Number skills can be tested by the familiar arithmetic problem, by checking paired lists of numbers to see which are alike and which are different, or by interpreting charts and graphs. In the latter test, a graph may be printed in the test booklet which you are asked to use as the basis for answering questions.

4) Observation
A popular test for law-enforcement positions is the observation test. A picture is shown to you for several minutes, then taken away. Questions about the picture test your ability to observe both details and larger elements.

5) Following directions
In many positions in the public service, the employee must be able to carry out written instructions dependably and accurately. You may be given a chart with several columns, each column listing a variety of information. The questions require you to carry out directions involving the information given in the chart.

6) Skills and aptitudes
Performance tests effectively measure some manual skills and aptitudes. When the skill is one in which you are trained, such as typing or shorthand, you can practice. These tests are often very much like those given in business school or high school courses. For many of the other skills and aptitudes, however, no short-time preparation can be made. Skills and abilities natural to you or that you have developed throughout your lifetime are being tested.

Many of the general questions just described provide all the data needed to answer the questions and ask you to use your reasoning ability to find the answers. Your best preparation for these tests, as well as for tests of facts and ideas, is to be at your physical and mental best. You, no doubt, have your own methods of getting into an exam-taking mood and keeping "in shape." The next section lists some ideas on this subject.

IV. KINDS OF QUESTIONS

Only rarely is the "essay" question, which you answer in narrative form, used in civil service tests. Civil service tests are usually of the short-answer type. Full instructions for answering these questions will be given to you at the examination. But in case this is your first experience with short-answer questions and separate answer sheets, here is what you need to know:

1) Multiple-choice Questions
Most popular of the short-answer questions is the "multiple choice" or "best answer" question. It can be used, for example, to test for factual knowledge, ability to solve problems or judgment in meeting situations found at work.
A multiple-choice question is normally one of three types—
- It can begin with an incomplete statement followed by several possible endings. You are to find the one ending which *best* completes the statement, although some of the others may not be entirely wrong.
- It can also be a complete statement in the form of a question which is answered by choosing one of the statements listed.

- It can be in the form of a problem – again you select the best answer.

Here is an example of a multiple-choice question with a discussion which should give you some clues as to the method for choosing the right answer:

When an employee has a complaint about his assignment, the action which will *best* help him overcome his difficulty is to
- A. discuss his difficulty with his coworkers
- B. take the problem to the head of the organization
- C. take the problem to the person who gave him the assignment
- D. say nothing to anyone about his complaint

In answering this question, you should study each of the choices to find which is best. Consider choice "A" – Certainly an employee may discuss his complaint with fellow employees, but no change or improvement can result, and the complaint remains unresolved. Choice "B" is a poor choice since the head of the organization probably does not know what assignment you have been given, and taking your problem to him is known as "going over the head" of the supervisor. The supervisor, or person who made the assignment, is the person who can clarify it or correct any injustice. Choice "C" is, therefore, correct. To say nothing, as in choice "D," is unwise. Supervisors have and interest in knowing the problems employees are facing, and the employee is seeking a solution to his problem.

2) True/False Questions

The "true/false" or "right/wrong" form of question is sometimes used. Here a complete statement is given. Your job is to decide whether the statement is right or wrong.

SAMPLE: A roaming cell-phone call to a nearby city costs less than a non-roaming call to a distant city.

This statement is wrong, or false, since roaming calls are more expensive.

This is not a complete list of all possible question forms, although most of the others are variations of these common types. You will always get complete directions for answering questions. Be sure you understand *how* to mark your answers – ask questions until you do.

V. RECORDING YOUR ANSWERS

Computer terminals are used more and more today for many different kinds of exams.

For an examination with very few applicants, you may be told to record your answers in the test booklet itself. Separate answer sheets are much more common. If this separate answer sheet is to be scored by machine – and this is often the case – it is highly important that you mark your answers correctly in order to get credit.

An electronic scoring machine is often used in civil service offices because of the speed with which papers can be scored. Machine-scored answer sheets must be marked with a pencil, which will be given to you. This pencil has a high graphite content which responds to the electronic scoring machine. As a matter of fact, stray dots may register as answers, so do not let your pencil rest on the answer sheet while you are pondering the correct answer. Also, if your pencil lead breaks or is otherwise defective, ask for another.

Since the answer sheet will be dropped in a slot in the scoring machine, be careful not to bend the corners or get the paper crumpled.

The answer sheet normally has five vertical columns of numbers, with 30 numbers to a column. These numbers correspond to the question numbers in your test booklet. After each number, going across the page are four or five pairs of dotted lines. These short dotted lines have small letters or numbers above them. The first two pairs may also have a "T" or "F" above the letters. This indicates that the first two pairs only are to be used if the questions are of the true-false type. If the questions are multiple choice, disregard the "T" and "F" and pay attention only to the small letters or numbers.

Answer your questions in the manner of the sample that follows:

32. The largest city in the United States is
    A. Washington, D.C.
    B. New York City
    C. Chicago
    D. Detroit
    E. San Francisco

1) Choose the answer you think is best. (New York City is the largest, so "B" is correct.)
2) Find the row of dotted lines numbered the same as the question you are answering. (Find row number 32)
3) Find the pair of dotted lines corresponding to the answer. (Find the pair of lines under the mark "B.")
4) Make a solid black mark between the dotted lines.

VI. BEFORE THE TEST

Common sense will help you find procedures to follow to get ready for an examination. Too many of us, however, overlook these sensible measures. Indeed, nervousness and fatigue have been found to be the most serious reasons why applicants fail to do their best on civil service tests. Here is a list of reminders:

- Begin your preparation early – Don't wait until the last minute to go scurrying around for books and materials or to find out what the position is all about.
- Prepare continuously – An hour a night for a week is better than an all-night cram session. This has been definitely established. What is more, a night a week for a month will return better dividends than crowding your study into a shorter period of time.
- Locate the place of the exam – You have been sent a notice telling you when and where to report for the examination. If the location is in a different town or otherwise unfamiliar to you, it would be well to inquire the best route and learn something about the building.
- Relax the night before the test – Allow your mind to rest. Do not study at all that night. Plan some mild recreation or diversion; then go to bed early and get a good night's sleep.
- Get up early enough to make a leisurely trip to the place for the test – This way unforeseen events, traffic snarls, unfamiliar buildings, etc. will not upset you.
- Dress comfortably – A written test is not a fashion show. You will be known by number and not by name, so wear something comfortable.

- Leave excess paraphernalia at home – Shopping bags and odd bundles will get in your way. You need bring only the items mentioned in the official notice you received; usually everything you need is provided. Do not bring reference books to the exam. They will only confuse those last minutes and be taken away from you when in the test room.
- Arrive somewhat ahead of time – If because of transportation schedules you must get there very early, bring a newspaper or magazine to take your mind off yourself while waiting.
- Locate the examination room – When you have found the proper room, you will be directed to the seat or part of the room where you will sit. Sometimes you are given a sheet of instructions to read while you are waiting. Do not fill out any forms until you are told to do so; just read them and be prepared.
- Relax and prepare to listen to the instructions
- If you have any physical problem that may keep you from doing your best, be sure to tell the test administrator. If you are sick or in poor health, you really cannot do your best on the exam. You can come back and take the test some other time.

VII. AT THE TEST

The day of the test is here and you have the test booklet in your hand. The temptation to get going is very strong. Caution! There is more to success than knowing the right answers. You must know how to identify your papers and understand variations in the type of short-answer question used in this particular examination. Follow these suggestions for maximum results from your efforts:

1) Cooperate with the monitor

The test administrator has a duty to create a situation in which you can be as much at ease as possible. He will give instructions, tell you when to begin, check to see that you are marking your answer sheet correctly, and so on. He is not there to guard you, although he will see that your competitors do not take unfair advantage. He wants to help you do your best.

2) Listen to all instructions

Don't jump the gun! Wait until you understand all directions. In most civil service tests you get more time than you need to answer the questions. So don't be in a hurry. Read each word of instructions until you clearly understand the meaning. Study the examples, listen to all announcements and follow directions. Ask questions if you do not understand what to do.

3) Identify your papers

Civil service exams are usually identified by number only. You will be assigned a number; you must not put your name on your test papers. Be sure to copy your number correctly. Since more than one exam may be given, copy your exact examination title.

4) Plan your time

Unless you are told that a test is a "speed" or "rate of work" test, speed itself is usually not important. Time enough to answer all the questions will be provided, but this does not mean that you have all day. An overall time limit has been set. Divide the total time (in minutes) by the number of questions to determine the approximate time you have for each question.

5) Do not linger over difficult questions

If you come across a difficult question, mark it with a paper clip (useful to have along) and come back to it when you have been through the booklet. One caution if you do this – be sure to skip a number on your answer sheet as well. Check often to be sure that you have not lost your place and that you are marking in the row numbered the same as the question you are answering.

6) Read the questions

Be sure you know what the question asks! Many capable people are unsuccessful because they failed to *read* the questions correctly.

7) Answer all questions

Unless you have been instructed that a penalty will be deducted for incorrect answers, it is better to guess than to omit a question.

8) Speed tests

It is often better NOT to guess on speed tests. It has been found that on timed tests people are tempted to spend the last few seconds before time is called in marking answers at random – without even reading them – in the hope of picking up a few extra points. To discourage this practice, the instructions may warn you that your score will be "corrected" for guessing. That is, a penalty will be applied. The incorrect answers will be deducted from the correct ones, or some other penalty formula will be used.

9) Review your answers

If you finish before time is called, go back to the questions you guessed or omitted to give them further thought. Review other answers if you have time.

10) Return your test materials

If you are ready to leave before others have finished or time is called, take ALL your materials to the monitor and leave quietly. Never take any test material with you. The monitor can discover whose papers are not complete, and taking a test booklet may be grounds for disqualification.

VIII. EXAMINATION TECHNIQUES

1) Read the general instructions carefully. These are usually printed on the first page of the exam booklet. As a rule, these instructions refer to the timing of the examination; the fact that you should not start work until the signal and must stop work at a signal, etc. If there are any *special* instructions, such as a choice of questions to be answered, make sure that you note this instruction carefully.

2) When you are ready to start work on the examination, that is as soon as the signal has been given, read the instructions to each question booklet, underline any key words or phrases, such as *least, best, outline, describe* and the like. In this way you will tend to answer as requested rather than discover on reviewing your paper that you *listed without describing*, that you selected the *worst* choice rather than the *best* choice, etc.

3) If the examination is of the objective or multiple-choice type – that is, each question will also give a series of possible answers: A, B, C or D, and you are called upon to select the best answer and write the letter next to that answer on your answer paper – it is advisable to start answering each question in turn. There may be anywhere from 50 to 100 such questions in the three or four hours allotted and you can see how much time would be taken if you read through all the questions before beginning to answer any. Furthermore, if you come across a question or group of questions which you know would be difficult to answer, it would undoubtedly affect your handling of all the other questions.

4) If the examination is of the essay type and contains but a few questions, it is a moot point as to whether you should read all the questions before starting to answer any one. Of course, if you are given a choice – say five out of seven and the like – then it is essential to read all the questions so you can eliminate the two that are most difficult. If, however, you are asked to answer all the questions, there may be danger in trying to answer the easiest one first because you may find that you will spend too much time on it. The best technique is to answer the first question, then proceed to the second, etc.

5) Time your answers. Before the exam begins, write down the time it started, then add the time allowed for the examination and write down the time it must be completed, then divide the time available somewhat as follows:
    - If 3-1/2 hours are allowed, that would be 210 minutes. If you have 80 objective-type questions, that would be an average of 2-1/2 minutes per question. Allow yourself no more than 2 minutes per question, or a total of 160 minutes, which will permit about 50 minutes to review.
    - If for the time allotment of 210 minutes there are 7 essay questions to answer, that would average about 30 minutes a question. Give yourself only 25 minutes per question so that you have about 35 minutes to review.

6) The most important instruction is to *read each question* and make sure you know what is wanted. The second most important instruction is to *time yourself properly* so that you answer every question. The third most important instruction is to *answer every question*. Guess if you have to but include something for each question. Remember that you will receive no credit for a blank and will probably receive some credit if you write something in answer to an essay question. If you guess a letter – say "B" for a multiple-choice question – you may have guessed right. If you leave a blank as an answer to a multiple-choice question, the examiners may respect your feelings but it will not add a point to your score. Some exams may penalize you for wrong answers, so in such cases *only*, you may not want to guess unless you have some basis for your answer.

7) Suggestions
    a. Objective-type questions
        1. Examine the question booklet for proper sequence of pages and questions
        2. Read all instructions carefully
        3. Skip any question which seems too difficult; return to it after all other questions have been answered
        4. Apportion your time properly; do not spend too much time on any single question or group of questions

5. Note and underline key words – *all, most, fewest, least, best, worst, same, opposite*, etc.
6. Pay particular attention to negatives
7. Note unusual option, e.g., unduly long, short, complex, different or similar in content to the body of the question
8. Observe the use of "hedging" words – *probably, may, most likely*, etc.
9. Make sure that your answer is put next to the same number as the question
10. Do not second-guess unless you have good reason to believe the second answer is definitely more correct
11. Cross out original answer if you decide another answer is more accurate; do not erase until you are ready to hand your paper in
12. Answer all questions; guess unless instructed otherwise
13. Leave time for review

b. Essay questions
1. Read each question carefully
2. Determine exactly what is wanted. Underline key words or phrases.
3. Decide on outline or paragraph answer
4. Include many different points and elements unless asked to develop any one or two points or elements
5. Show impartiality by giving pros and cons unless directed to select one side only
6. Make and write down any assumptions you find necessary to answer the questions
7. Watch your English, grammar, punctuation and choice of words
8. Time your answers; don't crowd material

8) Answering the essay question

Most essay questions can be answered by framing the specific response around several key words or ideas. Here are a few such key words or ideas:

M's: manpower, materials, methods, money, management
P's: purpose, program, policy, plan, procedure, practice, problems, pitfalls, personnel, public relations

a. Six basic steps in handling problems:
1. Preliminary plan and background development
2. Collect information, data and facts
3. Analyze and interpret information, data and facts
4. Analyze and develop solutions as well as make recommendations
5. Prepare report and sell recommendations
6. Install recommendations and follow up effectiveness

b. Pitfalls to avoid
1. *Taking things for granted* – A statement of the situation does not necessarily imply that each of the elements is necessarily true; for example, a complaint may be invalid and biased so that all that can be taken for granted is that a complaint has been registered

2. *Considering only one side of a situation* – Wherever possible, indicate several alternatives and then point out the reasons you selected the best one
3. *Failing to indicate follow up* – Whenever your answer indicates action on your part, make certain that you will take proper follow-up action to see how successful your recommendations, procedures or actions turn out to be
4. *Taking too long in answering any single question* – Remember to time your answers properly

IX. AFTER THE TEST

Scoring procedures differ in detail among civil service jurisdictions although the general principles are the same. Whether the papers are hand-scored or graded by machine we have described, they are nearly always graded by number. That is, the person who marks the paper knows only the number – never the name – of the applicant. Not until all the papers have been graded will they be matched with names. If other tests, such as training and experience or oral interview ratings have been given, scores will be combined. Different parts of the examination usually have different weights. For example, the written test might count 60 percent of the final grade, and a rating of training and experience 40 percent. In many jurisdictions, veterans will have a certain number of points added to their grades.

After the final grade has been determined, the names are placed in grade order and an eligible list is established. There are various methods for resolving ties between those who get the same final grade – probably the most common is to place first the name of the person whose application was received first. Job offers are made from the eligible list in the order the names appear on it. You will be notified of your grade and your rank as soon as all these computations have been made. This will be done as rapidly as possible.

People who are found to meet the requirements in the announcement are called "eligibles." Their names are put on a list of eligible candidates. An eligible's chances of getting a job depend on how high he stands on this list and how fast agencies are filling jobs from the list.

When a job is to be filled from a list of eligibles, the agency asks for the names of people on the list of eligibles for that job. When the civil service commission receives this request, it sends to the agency the names of the three people highest on this list. Or, if the job to be filled has specialized requirements, the office sends the agency the names of the top three persons who meet these requirements from the general list.

The appointing officer makes a choice from among the three people whose names were sent to him. If the selected person accepts the appointment, the names of the others are put back on the list to be considered for future openings.

That is the rule in hiring from all kinds of eligible lists, whether they are for typist, carpenter, chemist, or something else. For every vacancy, the appointing officer has his choice of any one of the top three eligibles on the list. This explains why the person whose name is on top of the list sometimes does not get an appointment when some of the persons lower on the list do. If the appointing officer chooses the second or third eligible, the No. 1 eligible does not get a job at once, but stays on the list until he is appointed or the list is terminated.

X. HOW TO PASS THE INTERVIEW TEST

The examination for which you applied requires an oral interview test. You have already taken the written test and you are now being called for the interview test – the final part of the formal examination.

You may think that it is not possible to prepare for an interview test and that there are no procedures to follow during an interview. Our purpose is to point out some things you can do in advance that will help you and some good rules to follow and pitfalls to avoid while you are being interviewed.

What is an interview supposed to test?

The written examination is designed to test the technical knowledge and competence of the candidate; the oral is designed to evaluate intangible qualities, not readily measured otherwise, and to establish a list showing the relative fitness of each candidate – as measured against his competitors – for the position sought. Scoring is not on the basis of "right" and "wrong," but on a sliding scale of values ranging from "not passable" to "outstanding." As a matter of fact, it is possible to achieve a relatively low score without a single "incorrect" answer because of evident weakness in the qualities being measured.

Occasionally, an examination may consist entirely of an oral test – either an individual or a group oral. In such cases, information is sought concerning the technical knowledges and abilities of the candidate, since there has been no written examination for this purpose. More commonly, however, an oral test is used to supplement a written examination.

Who conducts interviews?

The composition of oral boards varies among different jurisdictions. In nearly all, a representative of the personnel department serves as chairman. One of the members of the board may be a representative of the department in which the candidate would work. In some cases, "outside experts" are used, and, frequently, a businessman or some other representative of the general public is asked to serve. Labor and management or other special groups may be represented. The aim is to secure the services of experts in the appropriate field.

However the board is composed, it is a good idea (and not at all improper or unethical) to ascertain in advance of the interview who the members are and what groups they represent. When you are introduced to them, you will have some idea of their backgrounds and interests, and at least you will not stutter and stammer over their names.

What should be done before the interview?

While knowledge about the board members is useful and takes some of the surprise element out of the interview, there is other preparation which is more substantive. It *is* possible to prepare for an oral interview – in several ways:

1) Keep a copy of your application and review it carefully before the interview

This may be the only document before the oral board, and the starting point of the interview. Know what education and experience you have listed there, and the sequence and dates of all of it. Sometimes the board will ask you to review the highlights of your experience for them; you should not have to hem and haw doing it.

2) Study the class specification and the examination announcement

Usually, the oral board has one or both of these to guide them. The qualities, characteristics or knowledges required by the position sought are stated in these documents. They offer valuable clues as to the nature of the oral interview. For example, if the job involves supervisory responsibilities, the announcement will usually indicate that knowledge of modern supervisory methods and the qualifications of the candidate as a supervisor will be tested. If so, you can expect such questions, frequently in the form of a hypothetical situation which you are expected to solve. NEVER go into an oral without knowledge of the duties and responsibilities of the job you seek.

3) Think through each qualification required

Try to visualize the kind of questions you would ask if you were a board member. How well could you answer them? Try especially to appraise your own knowledge and background in each area, *measured against the job sought*, and identify any areas in which you are weak. Be critical and realistic – do not flatter yourself.

4) Do some general reading in areas in which you feel you may be weak

For example, if the job involves supervision and your past experience has NOT, some general reading in supervisory methods and practices, particularly in the field of human relations, might be useful. Do NOT study agency procedures or detailed manuals. The oral board will be testing your understanding and capacity, not your memory.

5) Get a good night's sleep and watch your general health and mental attitude

You will want a clear head at the interview. Take care of a cold or any other minor ailment, and of course, no hangovers.

What should be done on the day of the interview?

Now comes the day of the interview itself. Give yourself plenty of time to get there. Plan to arrive somewhat ahead of the scheduled time, particularly if your appointment is in the fore part of the day. If a previous candidate fails to appear, the board might be ready for you a bit early. By early afternoon an oral board is almost invariably behind schedule if there are many candidates, and you may have to wait. Take along a book or magazine to read, or your application to review, but leave any extraneous material in the waiting room when you go in for your interview. In any event, relax and compose yourself.

The matter of dress is important. The board is forming impressions about you – from your experience, your manners, your attitude, and your appearance. Give your personal appearance careful attention. Dress your best, but not your flashiest. Choose conservative, appropriate clothing, and be sure it is immaculate. This is a business interview, and your appearance should indicate that you regard it as such. Besides, being well groomed and properly dressed will help boost your confidence.

Sooner or later, someone will call your name and escort you into the interview room. *This is it.* From here on you are on your own. It is too late for any more preparation. But remember, you asked for this opportunity to prove your fitness, and you are here because your request was granted.

What happens when you go in?

The usual sequence of events will be as follows: The clerk (who is often the board stenographer) will introduce you to the chairman of the oral board, who will introduce you to the other members of the board. Acknowledge the introductions before you sit down. Do not be surprised if you find a microphone facing you or a stenotypist sitting by. Oral interviews are usually recorded in the event of an appeal or other review.

Usually the chairman of the board will open the interview by reviewing the highlights of your education and work experience from your application – primarily for the benefit of the other members of the board, as well as to get the material into the record. Do not interrupt or comment unless there is an error or significant misinterpretation; if that is the case, do not hesitate. But do not quibble about insignificant matters. Also, he will usually ask you some question about your education, experience or your present job – partly to get you to start talking and to establish the interviewing "rapport." He may start the actual questioning, or turn it over to one of the other members. Frequently, each member undertakes the questioning on a particular area, one in which he is perhaps most competent, so you can expect each member to participate in the examination. Because time is limited, you may also expect some rather abrupt switches in the direction the questioning takes, so do not be upset by it. Normally, a board member will not pursue a single line of questioning unless he discovers a particular strength or weakness.

After each member has participated, the chairman will usually ask whether any member has any further questions, then will ask you if you have anything you wish to add. Unless you are expecting this question, it may floor you. Worse, it may start you off on an extended, extemporaneous speech. The board is not usually seeking more information. The question is principally to offer you a last opportunity to present further qualifications or to indicate that you have nothing to add. So, if you feel that a significant qualification or characteristic has been overlooked, it is proper to point it out in a sentence or so. Do not compliment the board on the thoroughness of their examination – they have been sketchy, and you know it. If you wish, merely say, "No thank you, I have nothing further to add." This is a point where you can "talk yourself out" of a good impression or fail to present an important bit of information. Remember, *you close the interview yourself*.

The chairman will then say, "That is all, Mr. _____, thank you." Do not be startled; the interview is over, and quicker than you think. Thank him, gather your belongings and take your leave. Save your sigh of relief for the other side of the door.

How to put your best foot forward

Throughout this entire process, you may feel that the board individually and collectively is trying to pierce your defenses, seek out your hidden weaknesses and embarrass and confuse you. Actually, this is not true. They are obliged to make an appraisal of your qualifications for the job you are seeking, and they want to see you in your best light. Remember, they must interview all candidates and a non-cooperative candidate may become a failure in spite of their best efforts to bring out his qualifications. Here are 15 suggestions that will help you:

1) Be natural – Keep your attitude confident, not cocky

If you are not confident that you can do the job, do not expect the board to be. Do not apologize for your weaknesses, try to bring out your strong points. The board is interested in a positive, not negative, presentation. Cockiness will antagonize any board member and make him wonder if you are covering up a weakness by a false show of strength.

2) Get comfortable, but don't lounge or sprawl

Sit erectly but not stiffly. A careless posture may lead the board to conclude that you are careless in other things, or at least that you are not impressed by the importance of the occasion. Either conclusion is natural, even if incorrect. Do not fuss with your clothing, a pencil or an ashtray. Your hands may occasionally be useful to emphasize a point; do not let them become a point of distraction.

3) Do not wisecrack or make small talk

This is a serious situation, and your attitude should show that you consider it as such. Further, the time of the board is limited – they do not want to waste it, and neither should you.

4) Do not exaggerate your experience or abilities
In the first place, from information in the application or other interviews and sources, the board may know more about you than you think. Secondly, you probably will not get away with it. An experienced board is rather adept at spotting such a situation, so do not take the chance.

5) If you know a board member, do not make a point of it, yet do not hide it
Certainly you are not fooling him, and probably not the other members of the board. Do not try to take advantage of your acquaintanceship – it will probably do you little good.

6) Do not dominate the interview
Let the board do that. They will give you the clues – do not assume that you have to do all the talking. Realize that the board has a number of questions to ask you, and do not try to take up all the interview time by showing off your extensive knowledge of the answer to the first one.

7) Be attentive
You only have 20 minutes or so, and you should keep your attention at its sharpest throughout. When a member is addressing a problem or question to you, give him your undivided attention. Address your reply principally to him, but do not exclude the other board members.

8) Do not interrupt
A board member may be stating a problem for you to analyze. He will ask you a question when the time comes. Let him state the problem, and wait for the question.

9) Make sure you understand the question
Do not try to answer until you are sure what the question is. If it is not clear, restate it in your own words or ask the board member to clarify it for you. However, do not haggle about minor elements.

10) Reply promptly but not hastily
A common entry on oral board rating sheets is "candidate responded readily," or "candidate hesitated in replies." Respond as promptly and quickly as you can, but do not jump to a hasty, ill-considered answer.

11) Do not be peremptory in your answers
A brief answer is proper – but do not fire your answer back. That is a losing game from your point of view. The board member can probably ask questions much faster than you can answer them.

12) Do not try to create the answer you think the board member wants
He is interested in what kind of mind you have and how it works – not in playing games. Furthermore, he can usually spot this practice and will actually grade you down on it.

13) Do not switch sides in your reply merely to agree with a board member
Frequently, a member will take a contrary position merely to draw you out and to see if you are willing and able to defend your point of view. Do not start a debate, yet do not surrender a good position. If a position is worth taking, it is worth defending.

14) Do not be afraid to admit an error in judgment if you are shown to be wrong

The board knows that you are forced to reply without any opportunity for careful consideration. Your answer may be demonstrably wrong. If so, admit it and get on with the interview.

15) Do not dwell at length on your present job

The opening question may relate to your present assignment. Answer the question but do not go into an extended discussion. You are being examined for a *new* job, not your present one. As a matter of fact, try to phrase ALL your answers in terms of the job for which you are being examined.

Basis of Rating

Probably you will forget most of these "do's" and "don'ts" when you walk into the oral interview room. Even remembering them all will not ensure you a passing grade. Perhaps you did not have the qualifications in the first place. But remembering them will help you to put your best foot forward, without treading on the toes of the board members.

Rumor and popular opinion to the contrary notwithstanding, an oral board wants you to make the best appearance possible. They know you are under pressure – but they also want to see how you respond to it as a guide to what your reaction would be under the pressures of the job you seek. They will be influenced by the degree of poise you display, the personal traits you show and the manner in which you respond.

ABOUT THIS BOOK

This book contains tests divided into Examination Sections. Go through each test, answering every question in the margin. We have also attached a sample answer sheet at the back of the book that can be removed and used. At the end of each test look at the answer key and check your answers. On the ones you got wrong, look at the right answer choice and learn. Do not fill in the answers first. Do not memorize the questions and answers, but understand the answer and principles involved. On your test, the questions will likely be different from the samples. Questions are changed and new ones added. If you understand these past questions you should have success with any changes that arise. Tests may consist of several types of questions. We have additional books on each subject should more study be advisable or necessary for you. Finally, the more you study, the better prepared you will be. This book is intended to be the last thing you study before you walk into the examination room. Prior study of relevant texts is also recommended. NLC publishes some of these in our Fundamental Series. Knowledge and good sense are important factors in passing your exam. Good luck also helps. So now study this Passbook, absorb the material contained within and take that knowledge into the examination. Then do your best to pass that exam.

EXAMINATION SECTION

EXAMINATION SECTION
TEST 1

DIRECTIONS: Each question or incomplete statement is followed by several suggested answers or completions. Select the one that BEST answers the question or completes the statement. *PRINT THE LETTER OF THE CORRECT ANSWER IN THE SPACE AT THE RIGHT.*

1. Physical and mental health are essential to the officer. According to this statement, the officer MUST be

    A. as wise as he is strong
    B. smarter than most people
    C. sound in mind and body
    D. stronger than the average criminal

2. Teamwork is the basis of successful law enforcement. The factor stressed by this statement is

    A. cooperation   B. determination
    C. initiative   D. pride

3. Legal procedure is a means, not an end. Its function is merely to accomplish the enforcement of legal rights. A litigant has no vested interest in the observance of the rules of procedure as such. All that he should be entitled to demand is that he be given an opportunity for a fair and impartial trial of his case. He should not be permitted to invoke the aid of technical rules merely to embarrass his adversary.
   According to this paragraph, it is MOST correct to state that

    A. observance of the rules of procedure guarantees a fair trial
    B. embarrassment of an adversary through technical rules does not make a fair trial
    C. a litigant is not interested in the observance of rules of procedure
    D. technical rules must not be used in a trial

4. One theory states that all criminal behavior is taught by a process of communication within small intimate groups. An individual engages in criminal behavior if the number of criminal patterns which he has acquired exceed the number of non-criminal patterns. This statement indicates that criminal behavior is

    A. learned   B. instinctive
    C. hereditary   D. reprehensible

5. The law enforcement staff of today requires training and mental qualities of a high order. The poorly or partially prepared staff member lowers the standard of work, retards his own earning power, and fails in a career meant to provide a livelihood and social improvement.
   According to this statement,

    A. an inefficient member of a law enforcement staff will still earn a good livelihood
    B. law enforcement officers move in good social circles
    C. many people fail in law enforcement careers
    D. persons of training and ability are essential to a law enforcement staff

6. In any state, no crime can occur unless there is a written law forbidding the act or the omission in question, and even though an act may not be exactly in harmony with public policy, such act is not a crime unless it is expressly forbidden by legislative enactment.
According to the above statement,

   A. a crime is committed with reference to a particular law
   B. acts not in harmony with public policy should be forbidden by law
   C. non-criminal activity will promote public welfare
   D. legislative enactments frequently forbid actions in harmony with public policy

6.____

7. The unrestricted sale of firearms is one of the main causes of our shameful crime record. According to this statement, one of the causes of our crime record is

   A. development of firepower
   B. ease of securing weapons
   C. increased skill in using guns
   D. scientific perfection of firearms

7.____

8. Every person must be informed of the reason for his arrest unless he is arrested in the actual commission of a crime. Sufficient force to effect the arrest may be used, but the courts frown on brutal methods.
According to this statement, a person does NOT have to be informed of the reason for his arrest if

   A. brutal force was not used in effecting it
   B. the courts will later turn the defendant loose
   C. the person arrested knows force will be used if necessary
   D. the reason for it is clearly evident from the circumstances

8.____

9. An important duty of an officer is to keep order in the court.
On the basis of this statement, it is PROBABLY true that

   A. it is more important for an officer to be strong than it is for him to be smart
   B. people involved in court trials are noisy if not kept in check
   C. not every duty of an officer is important
   D. the maintenance of order is important for the proper conduct of court business

9.____

10. Ideally, a correctional system should include several types of institutions to provide different degrees of custody.
On the basis of this statement, one could MOST reasonably say that

   A. as the number of institutions in a correctional system increases, the efficiency of the system increases
   B. the difference in degree of custody for the inmate depends on the types of institutions in a correctional system
   C. the greater the variety of institutions, the stricter the degree of custody that can be maintained
   D. the same type of correctional institution is not desirable for the custody of all prisoners

10.____

11. The enforced idleness of a large percentage of adult men and women in our prisons is one of the direct causes of the tensions which burst forth in riot and disorder.
    On the basis of this statement, a good reason why inmates should perform daily work of some kind is that

    A. better morale and discipline can be maintained when inmates are kept busy
    B. daily work is an effective way of punishing inmates for the crimes they have committed
    C. law-abiding citizens must work, therefore, labor should also be required of inmates
    D. products of inmates' labor will in part pay the cost of their maintenance

11._____

12. With industry invading rural areas, the use of the automobile, and the speed of modern communications and transportation, the problems of neglect and delinquency are no longer peculiar to cities but an established feature of everyday life.
    This statement implies MOST directly that

    A. delinquents are moving from cities to rural areas
    B. delinquency and neglect are found in rural areas
    C. delinquency is not as much of a problem in rural areas as in cities
    D. rural areas now surpass cities in industry

12._____

13. Young men from minority groups, if unable to find employment, become discouraged and hopeless because of their economic position and may finally resort to any means of supplying their wants.
    The MOST reasonable of the following conclusions that may be drawn from this statement only is that

    A. discouragement sometimes leads to crime
    B. in general, young men from minority groups are criminals
    C. unemployment turns young men from crime
    D. young men from minority groups are seldom employed

13._____

14. To prevent crime, we must deal with the possible criminal long before he reaches the prison. Our aim should be not merely to reform the law breakers but to strike at the roots of crime: neglectful parents, bad companions, unsatisfactory homes, selfishness, disregard for the rights of others, and bad social conditions.
    The above statement recommends

    A. abolition of prisons   B. better reformatories
    C. compulsory education   D. general social reform

14._____

15. There is evidence which shows that comic books which glorify the criminal and criminal acts have a distinct influence in producing young criminals.
    According to this statement,

    A. comic books affect the development of criminal careers
    B. comic books specialize in reporting criminal acts
    C. young criminals read comic books exclusively
    D. young criminals should not be permitted to read comic books

15._____

16. Suppose a study shows that juvenile delinquents are equal in intelligence but three school grades behind juvenile non-delinquents.
On the basis of this information only, it is MOST reasonable to say that

    A. a delinquent usually progresses to the educational limit set by his intelligence
    B. educational achievement depends on intelligence only
    C. educational achievement is closely associated with delinquency
    D. lack of intelligence is closely associated with delinquency

17. There is no proof today that the experience of a prison sentence makes a better citizen of an adult. On the contrary, there seems some evidence that the experience is an unwholesome one that frequently confirms the criminality of the inmate.
From the above paragraph only, it may be BEST concluded that

    A. prison sentences tend to punish rather than rehabilitate
    B. all criminals should be given prison sentences
    C. we should abandon our penal institutions
    D. penal institutions are effective in rehabilitating criminals

18. Some courts are referred to as *criminal* courts while others are known as *civil* courts. This distinction in name is MOST probably based on the

    A. historical origin of the court
    B. link between the court and the police
    C. manner in which the judges are chosen
    D. type of cases tried there

19. Many children who are exposed to contacts and experiences of a delinquent nature become educated and trained in crime in the course of participating in the daily life of the neighborhood.
From this statement only, we may reasonably conclude that

    A. delinquency passes from parent to child
    B. neighborhood influences are usually bad
    C. schools are training grounds for delinquents
    D. none of the above conclusions is reasonable

20. Old age insurance, for whose benefits a quarter of a million city employees may elect to become eligible, is one feature of the Social Security Act that is wholly administered by the Federal government.
On the basis of this paragraph only, it may MOST reasonably be inferred that

    A. a quarter of a million city employees are drawing old age insurance
    B. a quarter of a million city employees have elected to become eligible for old age insurance
    C. the city has no part in administering Social Security old age insurance
    D. only the Federal government administers the Social Security Act

21. An officer's revolver is a defensive, and not offensive, weapon.
On the basis of this statement only, an officer should BEST draw his revolver to

    A. fire at an unarmed burglar
    B. force a suspect to confess
    C. frighten a juvenile delinquent
    D. protect his own life

22. Prevention of crime is of greater value to the community than the punishment of crime. If this statement is accepted as true, GREATEST emphasis should be placed on

    A. malingering B. medication
    C. imprisonment D. rehabilitation

23. The criminal is rarely or never reformed.
    Acceptance of this statement as true would mean that GREATEST emphasis should be placed on

    A. imprisonment B. parole
    C. probation D. malingering

24. The MOST accurate of the following statements about persons convicted of crimes is that

    A. their criminal behavior is almost invariably the result of low intelligence
    B. they are almost invariably legally insane
    C. they are more likely to come from underprivileged groups than from other groups
    D. they have certain facial characteristics which distinguish them from non-criminals

25. Suppose a study shows that the I.Q. (Intelligence Quotient) of prison inmates is 95 as opposed to an I.Q. of 100 for a numerically equivalent civilian group.
    A claim, on the basis of this study, that criminals have a lower I.Q. than non-criminals would be

    A. *improper;* prison inmates are criminals who have been caught
    B. *proper;* the study was numerically well done
    C. *improper;* the sample was inadequate
    D. *proper;* even misdemeanors are sometimes penalized by prison sentences

Questions 26-45.

DIRECTIONS: Select the letter of the word or expression that MOST NEARLY expresses the meaning of the capitalized word in the group.

26. ABDUCT

    A. lead B. kidnap C. sudden D. worthless

27. BIAS

    A. ability B. envy C. prejudice D. privilege

28. COERCE

    A. cancel B. force C. rescind D. rugged

29. CONDONE

    A. combine B. pardon C. revive D. spice

30. CONSISTENCY

    A. bravery B. readiness C. strain D. uniformity

31. CREDENCE
    A. belief   B. devotion   C. resemblance   D. tempo

32. CURRENT
    A. backward   B. brave   C. prevailing   D. wary

33. CUSTODY
    A. advisement   B. belligerence
    C. guardianship   D. suspicion

34. DEBILITY
    A. deceitfulness   B. decency
    C. strength   D. weakness

35. DEPLETE
    A. beg   B. empty   C. excuse   D. fold

36. ENUMERATE
    A. name one by one   B. disappear
    C. get rid of   D. pretend

37. FEIGN
    A. allow   B. incur   C. pretend   D. weaken

38. INSTIGATE
    A. analyze   B. coordinate   C. oppose   D. provoke

39. LIABLE
    A. careless   B. growing   C. mistaken   D. responsible

40. PONDER
    A. attack   B. heavy   C. meditate   D. solicit

41. PUGILIST
    A. farmer   B. politician
    C. prize fighter   D. stage actor

42. QUELL
    A. explode   B. inform   C. shake   D. suppress

43. RECIPROCAL
    A. mutual   B. organized   C. redundant   D. thoughtful

44. RUSE
    A. burn   B. impolite   C. rot   D. trick

45. STEALTHY   45._____

   A. crazed   B. flowing   C. sly   D. wicked

Questions 46-50.

DIRECTIONS: Each of the sentences numbered 46 to 50 may be classified under one of the following four categories:
    A faulty because of incorrect grammar
    B faulty because of incorrect punctuation
    C faulty because of incorrect capitalization or incorrect spelling
    D correct
Examine each sentence carefully to determine under which of the above four options it is best classified. Then, in the corresponding space at the right, write the letter preceding the option which is the BEST of the four suggested above. Each faulty sentence contains but one type of error. Consider a sentence to be correct if it contains none of the types of errors mentioned, even though there may be other correct ways of expressing the same thought.

46. They told both he and I that the prisoner had escaped.   46._____

47. Any superior officer, who, disregards the just complaints of his subordinates, is remiss in the performance of his duty.   47._____

48. Only those members of the national organization who resided in the Middle west attended the conference in Chicago.   48._____

49. We told him to give the investigation assignment to whoever was available.   49._____

50. Please do not disappoint and embarass us by not appearing in court.   50._____

KEY (CORRECT ANSWERS)

1. C	11. A	21. D	31. A	41. C
2. A	12. B	22. D	32. C	42. D
3. B	13. A	23. A	33. C	43. A
4. A	14. D	24. C	34. D	44. D
5. D	15. A	25. A	35. B	45. C
6. A	16. C	26. B	36. A	46. A
7. B	17. A	27. C	37. C	47. B
8. D	18. D	28. B	38. D	48. C
9. D	19. D	29. B	39. D	49. D
10. D	20. C	30. D	40. C	50. C

TEST 2

DIRECTIONS: Each question or incomplete statement is followed by several suggested answers or completions. Select the one that BEST answers the question or completes the statement. *PRINT THE LETTER OF THE CORRECT ANSWER IN THE SPACE AT THE RIGHT.*

1. Suppose a man falls from a two-story high scaffold and is unconscious. You should

   A. call for medical assistance and avoid moving the man
   B. get someone to help you move him indoors to a bed
   C. have someone help you walk him around until he revives
   D. hold his head up and pour a stimulant down his throat

   1.____

2. For proper first aid treatment, a person who has fainted should be

   A. doused with cold water and then warmly covered
   B. given artificial respiration until he is revived
   C. laid down with his head lower than the rest of his body
   D. slapped on the face until he is revived

   2.____

3. If you are called on to give first aid to a person who is suffering from shock, you should

   A. apply cold towels   B. give him a stimulant
   C. keep him awake   D. wrap him warmly

   3.____

4. Artificial respiration would NOT be proper first aid for a person suffering from

   A. drowning   B. electric shock
   C. external bleeding   D. suffocation

   4.____

5. Suppose you are called on to give first aid to several victims of an accident. FIRST attention should be given to the one who is

   A. bleeding severely   B. groaning loudly
   C. unconscious   D. vomiting

   5.____

6. If an officer's weekly salary is increased from $400.00 to $450.00, then the percent of increase is _____ percent.

   A. 10   B. 11 1/9   C. 12 1/2   D. 20

   6.____

7. Suppose that one-half the officers in a department have served for more than ten years, and one-third have served for more than 15 years.
Then, the fraction of officers who have served between ten and fifteen years is

   A. 1/3   B. 1/5   C. 1/6   D. 1/12

   7.____

8. In a city prison, there are four floors on which prisoners are housed. The top floor houses one-quarter of the inmates, the bottom floor houses one-sixth of the inmates, one-third are housed on the second floor. The rest of the inmates are housed on the third floor. If there are 90 inmates housed on the third floor, the total number of inmates housed on all four floors together is

   A. 270   B. 360   C. 450   D. 540

   8.____

9. Suppose that ten percent of those who commit serious crimes are convicted and that fifteen percent of those convicted are sentenced for more than 3 years.
   The percentage of those committing serious crimes who are sentenced for more than 3 years is _____ percent.

   A. 15   B. 1.5   C. .15   D. .015

10. Assume that there are 1,100 employees in a city agency. Of these, 15 percent are officers, 80 percent of whom are attorneys; of the attorneys, two-fifths have been with the agency over five years.
    Then the number of officers who are attorneys and have over five years' experience with the agency is MOST NEARLY

    A. 45   B. 53   C. 132   D. 165

11. An employee who has 500 cartons of supplies to pack can pack them at the rate of 50 an hour. After this employee has worked for half an hour, he is jointed by another employee who can pack 45 cartons an hour.
    Assuming that both employees can maintain their respective rates of speed, the total number of hours required to pack all the cartons is

    A. 4 1/2   B. 5   C. 5 1/2   D. 6 1/2

12. Thirty-six officers can complete an assignment in 22 days. Assuming that all officers work at the same rate of speed, the number of officers that would be needed to complete this assignment in 12 days is

    A. 42   B. 54   C. 66   D. 72

Questions 13-15.

DIRECTIONS: Questions 13 through 15, inclusive, are to be answered on the basis of the table below. Data for certain categories have been omitted from the You are to calculate the missing numbers if needed to answer the questions.

	2007	2008	Numerical Increase
Correction Officers	1,226	1,347	
Court Officers		529	34
Deputy Sheriffs	38	40	
Supervisors			
	2,180	2,414	

13. The number in the *Supervisors* group in 2007 was MOST NEARLY

    A. 500   B. 475   C. 450   D. 425

14. The LARGEST percentage increase from 2007 to 2008 was in the group of

    A. Correction officers   B. Court officers
    C. Deputy sheriffs   D. Supervisors

15. In 2008, the ratio of the number of Correction Officers to the total of the other three categories of employees was MOST NEARLY

    A. 1:1   B. 2:1   C. 3:1   D. 4:1

16. A directed verdict is made by a court when 16.____

    A. the facts are not disputed
    B. the defendant's motion for a directed verdict has been denied
    C. there is no question of law involved
    D. neither party has moved for a directed verdict

17. Papers on appeal of a criminal case do NOT include one of the following: 17.____

    A. Summons   B. Minutes of trial
    C. Complaint   D. Intermediate motion papers

18. A pleading titled *Smith vs. Jones, et al.* indicates 18.____

    A. two plaintiffs   B. two defendants
    C. more than two defendants   D. unknown defendants

19. A District Attorney makes a *prima facie* case when 19.____

    A. there is proof of guilt beyond a reasonable doubt
    B. the evidence is sufficient to convict in the absence of rebutting evidence
    C. the prosecution presents more evidence than the defense
    D. the defendant fails to take the stand

20. A person is NOT qualified to act as a trial juror in a criminal action if he or she 20.____

    A. has been convicted previously of a misdemeanor
    B. is under 18 years of age
    C. has scruples against the death penalty
    D. does not own property of a value at least $500

21. A court clerk who falsifies a court record commits a(n) 21.____

    A. misdemeanor
    B. offense
    C. felony
    D. no crime, but automatically forfeits his tenure

22. Insolent and contemptuous behavior to a judge during a court of record proceeding is punishable as 22.____

    A. civil contempt   B. criminal contempt
    C. disorderly conduct   D. a disorderly person

23. Offering a bribe to a court clerk would not constitute a crime UNLESS the 23.____

    A. court clerk accepted the bribe
    B. bribe consisted of money
    C. bribe was given with intent to influence the court clerk in his official functions
    D. court was actually in session

24. A defendant comes to trial in the same court in which he had previously been defendant in a similar case. 24.____
    The court officer should

    A. tell him, *Knew we'd be seeing you again*
    B. tell newspaper reporters what he knows of the previous action

C. treat him the same as he would any other defendant
D. warn the judge that the man had previously been a defendant

25. Suppose in conversation with you, an attorney strongly criticizes a ruling of the judge, and you believe the attorney to be correct.
You should

   A. assure him you feel the same way
   B. tell him the judge knows the law
   C. tell him to ask for an exception
   D. refuse to discuss the matter

25.____

26. Suppose a doorman refuses to admit you to an apartment house in which you are attempting to serve a process on a tenant.
Of the following, the BEST action for you to take is to

   A. bribe the doorman to admit you
   B. discard the process since it cannot be served
   C. gain entrance by force
   D. report the matter to your superior

26.____

27. False arrest is an offense for which the deputy sheriff may be held liable.
Therefore, before making an arrest, the deputy sheriff should

   A. be sure a witness is present
   B. be sure it is legal
   C. seek assistance from a patrolman
   D. deputize a private citizen

27.____

28. An arrested person should not be transported upon a public conveyance such as a streetcar, subway, or bus, except in an extreme emergency.
The reason for this regulation is MOST probably the

   A. danger of escape   B. embarrassment to the prisoner
   C. expense involved   D. possible delays

28.____

29. Except in rare emergencies, a deputy should not attempt to make an arrest without a partner.
The BEST reason for this is that the partner may be needed to

   A. arbitrate the matter
   B. lend prestige to the sheriff's office
   C. overcome resistance
   D. provide company for the deputy

29.____

30. At the end of each month, the deputy sheriff must submit to his superior officer an activity report covering the status of his assignments and the extent of his activities in the service of process during the month.
It is MOST important that such report be

   A. accurate   B. brief
   C. grammatically correct   D. lengthy

30.____

31. Deputies are required to hold seized chattels for three days after service of the replevin papers. This means three full 24-hour days, exclusive of the day of service, and the property should not be turned over earlier than 12:01 A.M. on the fourth day. When one day of the period falls on a Sunday or a public holiday, that day is excluded and an additional day must be added to make up the three.
According to this statement only, if service of replevin papers is made on Thursday, June 23rd, the property should be turned over on

    A. Sunday, June 26th
    B. Monday, June 27th
    C. Tuesday, June 28th
    D. Wednesday, June 29th

32. Certain property is declared by law to be exempt from seizure to satisfy a debt because it is of importance to the comfort of the family, although of small money On the basis of this law, which of the following would you MOST expect to be exempt from seizure?

    A. Broadloom rug
    B. Dining table
    C. Marble statuette
    D. Modern painting

33. As a general rule, a deputy sheriff is justified in refusing to seize an article which differs from the description in the replevin papers, unless the difference is clearly unimportant in the light of other identifying facts. According to this statement, which of the following would a deputy sheriff BEST be justified in seizing where there is a difference from the description in the papers?
A(n)

    A. automobile corresponding in make, year, model, and engine number, but differing in color
    B. sofa corresponding in upholstery material, color, width, and height, but differing in length
    C. television set corresponding in year, model, and size of screen, but differing in number of tubes required
    D. typewriter corresponding in year, model, size of type, and color, but differing in name of manufacturer

34. The legal aspect of the sheriff's duties is emphasized by his unique personal liability, not only for his own acts and omissions, but also for those of any deputy or employee in his office.
According to the foregoing quotation, it would be MOST correct to state that the sheriff

    A. and his employees have unique legal duties to perform
    B. is held responsible for actions taken by his subordinates
    C. is liable for the acts of his employees only under unique circumstances
    D. must personally serve many legal papers

35. Which one of the following descriptions of a defendant would help MOST in identifying him?

    A. Age - 31 years; weight - 168 pounds
    B. At time of escape was wearing gray hat, dark overcoat
    C. Deep scar running from left ear to chin
    D. Height - 5 feet, 9 inches; complexion - sallow

36. Which of the following could a deputy sheriff BEST accept as proof of a man's identity? 36._____

    A. A personal letter
    B. Automobile driver's license
    C. Automobile registration certificate
    D. Social security card

37. It was formerly the practice to require someone who knew the defendant by sight to accompany the deputy sheriff. It has been learned through experience that the value of such identification is over-rated. 37._____
From this paragraph only, it may be BEST inferred that

    A. circumstantial evidence is not reliable
    B. identifications are sometimes inaccurate
    C. people are usually for the underdog
    D. testimony is often contradictory

38. The depositions must set forth the facts tending to establish that an illegal act was committed and that the defendant is guilty. 38._____
According to this statement only, the one of the following which need NOT be included in a deposition is evidence that establishes the

    A. fact that an illegal act was committed
    B. fact that defendant committed the illegal act
    C. guilt of the defendant
    D. method of commission of the illegal act

39. Each deputy sheriff should understand how his own work helps to accomplish the purpose of the entire agency. 39._____
This statement means MOST NEARLY that the deputy sheriff should understand the

    A. efficiency of a small agency
    B. importance of his own job
    C. necessity for initiative
    D. value of a large organization

40. When X is accused of having cheated Y of a sum of money and Y is proven to have been deprived of the money, there is an additional requirement for a verdict against X. 40._____
The additional requirement is to prove that

    A. the money was stolen from Y
    B. X had the money after Y had it
    C. X had the money before Y had it
    D. X cheated Y of the money

41. To gain a verdict against X in a trial, it was necessary to show that he could have been at Y Street at 5 P.M. 41._____
It was proven that he was seen at Z Street at 4:45 P.M. The question that MUST be answered to show whether X is guilty is:

    A. How long does it take to get from Z Street to Y Street?
    B. In what sort of neighborhood is Z Street located?
    C. Was X acting suspiciously on the day in question?
    D. Who was with X when he was seen at Z Street at 4:45 P.M.?

42. The deputy sheriff must give the defendant reasonable time to secure the bail fixed in the process before confining him to jail.
    The CHIEF purpose of bail is to

    A. permit personnel to act as bondsmen
    B. permit the defendant his liberty while assuring his presence at the trial
    C. raise additional money for the general fund of the city treasury
    D. relieve the city of the necessity of bringing the defendant before a judge

43. When a jury is selected, the attorney for each side has a right to refuse to accept a certain number of prospective jurors without giving any reason therefor.
    The reason for this is MAINLY that

    A. attorneys can exclude persons likely to be biased even though no prejudice is admitted
    B. persons who will suffer economically by being summoned for jury duty can be excused forthwith
    C. relatives of the litigants can be excused, thus insuring a fair trial for each side
    D. there will be a greater number of people from which the jury can be selected, thus insuring better quality

44. Suppose a deputy sheriff, feeling that the verdict against a judgment debtor was unfair, permits him to escape.
    On the basis of this information only, it is safe to assume that the

    A. judge passing sentence was unduly harsh
    B. judgment debtor had possession of a large sum of money
    C. deputy sheriff was recently appointed
    D. deputy sheriff used poor judgment

45. A deputy sheriff shall not receive a gift from any defendant or other person on the defendant's behalf.
    The BEST explanation for this departmental rule is that

    A. acceptance of a gift has no significance
    B. favors may be expected in return
    C. gifts are only an expression of good will
    D. litigants cannot usually afford gifts

46. All concerned are MOST likely to recognize the deputy sheriff's authority and cooperate with him if he conveys by his manner a complete confidence that they will do so. According to this statement only, a deputy sheriff should display

    A. arrogance   B. agitation   C. assurance   D. excitement

47. Since he is a city employee, a deputy sheriff who refuses to waive immunity from prosecution when called on to testify in court automatically terminates his employment.
    From this statement only, it may be BEST inferred that

    A. a deputy sheriff is a city employee
    B. all city employees are deputy sheriffs
    C. city employees may be fired only for malfeasance
    D. deputy sheriffs who waive immunity may not be prosecuted

48. In one case, a mistrial was declared because the indictment used the pronoun *he* instead of *she*.
    The MOST useful information a deputy sheriff can derive from this statement is that

    A. accuracy is important
    B. mistrial is a legal term
    C. one must always use good grammar
    D. to misrepresent is felonious

49. It is desirable that a deputy sheriff acquire a knowledge of the procedures of the division to which he is assigned MAINLY because such knowledge will help him

    A. become familiar with anti-social behavior
    B. discharge his duties properly
    C. gain insight into causes of crime
    D. in any personal legal proceeding

50. It is a frequent misconception that deputy sheriffs can be recruited from those registers established for the recruitment of police officers or firefighters. While it is true that many common qualifications are found in all of these, specific standards for a sheriff's work are indicated, varying with the size, geographical location and policies of the office.
    According to this paragraph only, it may BEST be inferred that

    A. a successful deputy sheriff must have some qualifications not required of a policeman or fireman
    B. qualifications which make a successful patrolman will also make a successful fireman
    C. the same qualifications are required of a deputy sheriff regardless of the office to which he is assigned
    D. the successful deputy sheriff is required to be both more intelligent and stronger than a fireman

KEY (CORRECT ANSWERS)

1. A	11. C	21. C	31. C	41. A
2. C	12. C	22. B	32. B	42. B
3. D	13. D	23. C	33. A	43. A
4. C	14. D	24. C	34. B	44. D
5. A	15. A	25. D	35. C	45. B
6. C	16. A	26. D	36. B	46. C
7. C	17. D	27. B	37. B	47. A
8. B	18. C	28. A	38. D	48. A
9. B	19. B	29. C	39. B	49. B
10. B	20. B	30. A	40. D	50. A

SOLUTIONS TO PROBLEMS

6. CORRECT ANSWER: C

   $\dfrac{50}{400} = \dfrac{1}{8} = 12\dfrac{1}{2}\%$

7. CORRECT ANSWER: C

   $1/2 + 1/3 = 3/6 + 2/6 = 5/6$

   $\therefore 1 - 5/6 = 1/6$

8. CORRECT ANSWER: B

   $1/4 + 1/6 + 1/3 = 3/12 + 2/12 + 4/12 = 9/12 = 3/4$

   $\therefore$ 1 - 3/4 = 1/4 (rest of inmates housed on the third floor) Since 90 = 1/4, therefore, 4/4 (or 1) = 360.

9. CORRECT ANSWER: B

   .10 x .15 = .0150 = 1.5%

10. CORRECT ANSWER: B

    Step (1)
    ```
         1100
         x.15
         5500
         1100
       165.00 (peace officers)
    ```

    Step (2)
    ```
          165
         x.80
       132.00 (attorneys)
    ```

    Step (3)   132 x 2/5 = 264/5 = 52.8 (peace officers who are attorneys and have over five years' experience with the agency)

11. CORRECT ANSWER: C

    Since the first employee worked for 1/2 hour, he packed 25 cartons (50 ÷ 2). This leaves 475 cartons to be packed. This first employee packs at the rate of 50 an hour. The second employee, who joins him after 1/2 hour, packs at the rate of 45 an hour. 50 + 45 = 95 (rate of both employees together)

    $\therefore$ 475 ÷ 95 = 5 hours (time it takes both employees together) 5 hours + 1/2 hour = 5 1/2 hours

12. CORRECT ANSWER: C

    x : 36 = 22:12
    12 × x = 36 × 22
       12 x = 792
          x = 66

EXAMINATION SECTION
TEST 1

DIRECTIONS: Each question or incomplete statement is followed by several suggested answers or completions. Select the one that BEST answers the question or completes the statement. *PRINT THE LETTER OF THE CORRECT ANSWER IN THE SPACE AT THE RIGHT.*

1. As a sheriff, you have encountered certain problems in your work and have repeatedly sought help from your immediate superior. This superior has not responded to your appeals for problem-solving. Under the circumstances, it is GENERALLY advisable to

    A. solve your problems as best you can, making certain you cover yourself in the event of failure by keeping a detailed record of the number of times you requested help and were ignored
    B. bypass your immediate superior and seek a relationship with someone above his position after informing your immediate superior of your intention
    C. keep trying to obtain help from your immediate superior, secure in the knowledge that, because of your persistence, you have established a legitimate excuse for making mistakes
    D. ignore difficult problems, concentrating on those matters you can satisfactorily resolve

    1.____

2. As a sheriff, you have noticed that your deputy sheriff partner has developed some negative attitudes toward certain aspects of his work. Under the circumstances, it is BEST generally to

    A. show understanding and provide your partner with relevant information
    B. urge your partner to change his point of view immediately or face disciplinary action
    C. inform your superior that you have a trouble-maker on your hands and recommend suitable disciplinary action
    D. leave your partner alone and allow his views to change

    2.____

3. As a sheriff, you have told your deputy sheriff partner that he has made an error of judgment in his work. Your partner blames you for the lapse and complains about you to your superior. When you are questioned by your superior, it is MOST advisable to

    A. call attention to your greater experience, and carefully explain how the lapse was really the deputy sheriff's fault
    B. seek to provide data for a rational diagnosis of the matter
    C. deny responsibility, and show how you *go by the book*
    D. present a documented report of the deputy sheriff's incompetence and insubordination

    3.____

4. Assume that you are a senior deputy sheriff teamed with an inexperienced deputy sheriff. He is executing a seizure levy and has failed to take a satisfactory inventory. Both of you are still on the defendant's premises. In the circumstances, it is BEST to

    4.____

A. redo the inventory with the deputy sheriff, explaining how to avoid similar errors in the future
B. redo the inventory yourself, explaining that the office of the sheriff can't afford errors
C. make certain that the deputy sheriff understands that the error was his fault, then have him redo the inventory to your satisfaction
D. chastise the deputy sheriff privately and inform him that anyone who can't properly inventory shouldn't be a deputy sheriff

5. Anticipating difficulty from a possibly troublesome defendant on an arrest case, you, as a senior deputy sheriff, have instructed your partner, an inexperienced deputy sheriff, to observe your behavior on this assignment and not to participate, except in case of extreme need for assistance. The defendant assaults you as you attempt to make the arrest, and it is only with difficulty that you overcome the assault and make the arrest. Your partner observes all this and does not interfere. In your report on the incident, you state that your partner failed to exercise judgment and initiative in coming to your assistance. When confronted with your statement, your partner claims that he was following explicit instructions and that, in his view, no real need for his assistance existed. The MOST reasonable comment on the above incident is that the 5.____

A. deputy sheriff displayed a lack of initiative and cooperation
B. senior deputy sheriff gave conflicting orders, assuming understanding on the part of the deputy sheriff
C. deputy sheriff showed good judgment in not properly interpreting the senior deputy sheriff's instructions
D. senior deputy sheriff's instructions should have been given in writing, not orally

Questions 6-10.

DIRECTIONS: Questions 6 through 10 are to be answered only on the basis of the information contained in the table on the next page.

DISTRIBUTION OF CITIZENS' RESPONSES TO STATEMENTS CONCERNING SHERIFFS' ARRESTS

(Number of citizens responding = 1171)

	CATEGORIES				
	(A) Strongly Agree	(B) Agree	(C) Disagree	(D) Strongly Disagree	(E) Don't Know
I. Sheriffs act improperly in arresting defendants, even when these persons are rude and ill-mannered	12%	37%	36%	9%	6%
II. Sheriffs frequently use more force than necessary when making arrests	9%	19%	46%	19%	7%
III. Any defendant who insults or physically abuses a sheriff has no complaint if he is sternly handled in return	13%	44%	32%	7%	4%

6. The total percentage of responses to Statement III OTHER THAN *Strongly Agree* and *Disagree* is

   A. 45%   B. 46%   C. 55%   D. 59%

7. The number of *Disagree* responses to Statement II is MOST NEARLY

   A. 71   B. 114   C. 539   D. 820

8. Assume that for Statement II the (B) percentage of responses were doubled and the (A) percentage increased one and a half times. If the (D) and (E) percentages remained the same, the (C) percentage would then be MOST NEARLY

   A. 23%   B. 26%   C. 39%   D. 52%

9. The total number of *Don't Know* responses is MOST NEARLY

   A. 17
   B. 188
   C. 200
   D. a figure which cannot be determined from the table

10. If the percentage of *Disagree* responses to Statement III were 35% less, the resulting percentage would be MOST NEARLY

    A. 11%   B. 14%   C. 15%   D. 21%

Questions 11-15.

DIRECTIONS: Questions 11 through 15 are to be answered SOLELY on the basis of the following reading selection.

In studying the relationships of people to the organizational structure, it is absolutely necessary to identify and recognize the informal organizational structure. These relationships are necessary when coordination of a plan is attempted. They may be with *the boss,* line supervisors, staff personnel, or other representatives of the formal organization's hierarchy, and they may include the *liaison men* who serve as the leaders of the informal organization. An acquaintanceship with the people serving in these roles in the organization, and its formal counterpart, permits a supervisor to recognize sensitive areas in which it is simple to get a conflict reaction. Avoidance of such areas, plus conscious efforts to inform other people of his own objectives for various plans, will usually enlist their aid and support. Planning *without people* can lead to disaster because the individuals who must act together to make any plan a success are more important than the plans themselves.

11. Of the following titles, the one that MOST clearly describes the paragraph is

    A. Coordination of a Function
    B. Avoidance of Conflict
    C. Planning with People
    D. Planning Objectives

12. According to the paragraph, attempts at coordinating plans may fail unless

    A. the plan's objectives are clearly set forth
    B. conflict between groups is resolved

C. the plans themselves are worthwhile
D. informal relationships are recognized

13. According to the paragraph, conflict

    A. may, in some cases, be desirable to secure results
    B. produces more heat than light
    C. should be avoided at all costs
    D. possibilities can be predicted by a sensitive supervisor

14. The paragraph implies that

    A. informal relationships are more important than formal structure
    B. the weakness of a formal structure depends upon informal relationships
    C. liaison men are the key people to consult when taking formal and informal structures into account
    D. individuals in a group are at least as important as the plans for the group

15. The paragraph suggests that

    A. some planning can be disastrous
    B. certain people in sensitive areas should be avoided
    C. the supervisor should discourage acquaintanceships in the organization
    D. organizational relationships should be consciously limited

Questions 16-20.

DIRECTIONS: Questions 16 through 20 are sentences taken from reports on the administration of the office of the sheriff. Some are correct according to ordinary formal usage. Others are incorrect because they contain errors in English usage, spelling, or punctuation. Consider a sentence correct if it contains no errors in English usage, spelling, or punctuation, even if there may be other ways of writing the sentence correctly. Mark your answer:
   A. if sentence I only is correct
   B. if sentence II only is correct
   C. if sentences I and II are correct
   D. if neither sentence I nor II is correct.

16. I. A deputy sheriff must ascertain whether the debtor, has any property.
    II. A good deputy sheriff does not cause histerical excitement when he executes a process.

17. I. Having learned that he has been assigned a judgment debtor, the deputy sheriff should call upon him.
    II. The deputy sheriff may seize and remove property without requiring a bond.

18. I. If legal procedures are not observed, the resulting contract is not enforseable.
    II. If the directions from the creditor's attorney are not in writing, the deputy sheriff should request a letter of instructions from the attorney.

19. I. The deputy sheriff may confer with the defendant and may enter this defendants' place of business.
    II. A deputy sheriff must ascertain from the creditor's attorney whether the debtor has any property against which he may proceede.

19._____

20. I. The sheriff has a right to do whatever is reasonably necessary for the purpose of executing the order of the court.
    II. The written order of the court gives the sheriff general authority and he is governed in his acts by a very simple principal.

20._____

KEY (CORRECT ANSWERS)

1.	B		11.	C
2.	A		12.	D
3.	B		13.	D
4.	A		14.	D
5.	B		15.	A
6.	C		16.	D
7.	C		17.	C
8.	A		18.	B
9.	C		19.	D
10.	D		20.	A

TEST 2

DIRECTIONS: Each question or incomplete statement is followed by several suggested answers or completions. Select the one that BEST answers the question or completes the statement. *PRINT THE LETTER OF THE CORRECT ANSWER IN THE SPACE AT THE RIGHT.*

Questions 1-5.

DIRECTIONS: Questions 1 through 5 are to be answered SOLELY on the basis of the following reading selection.

The dynamics of group behavior may be summed up by saying that the individuals in a group respond to many lines of force arising out of their relationship with every other member of a group, and with the group itself. In addition, each member of a group quite naturally brings with him all the things that have been *bugging* him. Then, the situation or the setting in which the group meets, as well as the circumstances related to the formation of the group, are active working forces exerting some X influence upon each member of the group. Lastly, all of this kinetic energy is at the control of the person seeking to lead the group into some kind of action. If he is to produce something meaningful with the members of a group, he must utilize this energy, contain it, dissipate it in some fashion or be faced with difficulty.

This dynamic force inherent in any group can be harnessed by a supervisor with leadership qualities, but it must be controlled. It will not be contained by acting without consultation with group members, by refusing to accept suggestions coming from the group, or by refusing to explain or even give notice of contemplated actions. However, it can be controlled by placing the focus upon the members of the group, rather than upon the supervisor, and depending upon the leader-supervisor to provide as many participative experiences for group members as is commensurate with his own decision-making responsibilities. It is true that this is subordinate-centered leadership, but the supervisor can gain strength through permissive leadership without sacrificing basic responsibilities for effective planning and adequate control of operations.

1. Of the following titles, the one that MOST closely describes the reading selection is   1.____

    A. The Supervisor with Dynamic Leadership Potential
    B. Dissipation of Group Energy
    C. Controlling Group Relationships
    D. Sacrificing Basic Responsibilities

2. According to the reading selection, the setting in which the group meets   2.____

    A. can readily be modified either in whole or in part
    B. must be made meaningful in some fashion to foster skills development
    C. can provide the sole source of group dynamics
    D. is one of the forces exerting influence on group members

3. According to the selection, the members of the group   3.____

    A. should control their formation and development
    B. should control the circumstances of their meeting

C. are influenced by the forces creating the group
D. dissipate meaningless energy

4. According to the selection, the effective group leader 4.____

   A. controls the focus of the group
   B. focuses his control over the group
   C. controls group forces by focusing upon group members
   D. focuses the group's forces upon himself

5. According to the selection, effective leadership consists in 5.____

   A. partially compromising decision-making responsibilities
   B. partially sacrificing some basic responsibilities
   C. sometimes cultivating permissive subordinates
   D. providing participation for members of the group consistent with decision-making imperatives

Questions 6-10.

DIRECTIONS: Questions 6 through 10 consist of one sentence each. Each sentence contains an incorrectly used word. First, decide which is the incorrectly used word. Then, from among the options given, decide which word, when substituted for the incorrectly used word, makes the meaning of the sentence clear.

For Example: The U.S. national income exhibits a pattern of long term deflection.
   A. reflection   B. subjection
   C. rejoicing   D. growth

The word *deflection* in the sentence does not convey the meaning the sentence evidently intended to convey. The word *growth* (answer D) when substituted for the word *deflection* makes the meaning of the sentence clear. Accordingly, the answer to the question is D.

6. The study commissioned by the joint committee fell compassionately short of the mark and would have to be redone. 6.____

   A. successfully   B. insignificantly
   C. experimentally   D. woefully

7. He will not idly exploit any violation of the provisions of the order. 7.____

   A. tolerate   B. refuse   C. construe   D. guard

8. The defendant refused to be virile and bitterly protested service. 8.____

   A. irked   B. feasible C. docile   D. credible

9. As today's violence has no single cause, so its causes have no single scheme. 9.____

   A. deference   B. cure   C. flaw   D. relevance

10. He took the position that the success of the program was insidious on getting additional revenue.   10._____

    A. reputed   B. contingent
    C. failure   D. indeterminate

Questions 11-15.

DIRECTIONS: Each of Questions 11 through 15 consists of a statement containing five words in capital letters. One of these words in capital letters is not in keeping with the meaning which the statement is evidently intended to carry. The five words in capital letters in each statement are reprinted after the statement. Print the letter preceding the one of the five words which does most to spoil the true meaning of the statement in the space at the right.

11. Within each major DIVISION in a properly set up public or private organization, provision is made so that each NECESSARY activity is CARED for and lines of AUTHORITY and responsibility are clear-cut and INFINITE.   11._____

    A. division   B. necessary   C. cared
    D. authority   E. infinite

12. In public service, the scale of salaries paid must be INCIDENTAL to the services rendered, with due CONSIDERATION for the attraction of the desired MANPOWER and for the MAINTENANCE of a standard of living COMMENSURATE with the work to be performed.   12._____

    A. incidental   B. consideration   C. manpower
    D. maintenance   E. commensurate

13. An understanding of the AIMS of an organization by the staff will AID greatly in increasing the DEMAND of the correspondence work of the office, and will to a large extent DETERMINE the NATURE of the correspondence.   13._____

    A. aims   B. aid   C. demand
    D. determine   E. nature

14. BECAUSE the Civil Service Commission strongly feels that the MERIT system is a key factor in the MAINTENANCE of democratic government, it has adopted as one of its major DEFENSES the progressive democratization of its own PROCEDURES in dealing with candidates for positions in the public service.   14._____

    A. Because   B. merit   C. maintenance
    D. defenses   E. procedures

15. Retirement and pension systems are ESSENTIAL not only to provide employees with a means of support in the future, but also to prevent longevity and CHARITABLE considerations from UPSETTING the PROMOTIONAL opportunities for RETIRED members of the career service.   15._____

    A. essential   B. charitable   C. upsetting
    D. promotional   E. retired

Questions 16-20.

DIRECTIONS: Questions 16 through 20 are sentences taken from reports on the administration of the office of the sheriff. Some are correct according to ordinary formal usage. Others are incorrect because they contain errors in English usage, spelling or punctuation. Consider a sentence correct if it contains no errors in English usage, spelling or punctuation even if there may be other ways of writing the sentence correctly. Mark your answer:
- A. if sentence I only is correct
- B. if sentence II only is correct
- C. if sentences I and II are correct
- D. if neither sentence I nor II is correct.

16. I. If a deputy sheriff finds that property he has to attach is located on a ship, he should notify his supervisor.
    II. Any contract that tends to interfere with the administration of justice is illegal.

17. I. A mandate or official order of the court to the sheriff or other officer directs it to take into possession property of the judgment debtor.
    II. Tenancies from month-to-month, week-to-week, and sometimes year-to-year are termenable.

18. I. A civil arrest is an arrest pursuant to an order issued by a court in civil litigation.
    II. In a criminal arrest, a defendant is arrested for a crime he is alleged to have committed.

19. I. Having taken a defendant into custody, there is a complete restraint of personal liberty.
    II. Actual force is unnecessary when a deputy sheriff makes an arrest.

20. I. When a husband breaches a separation agreement by failing to supply to the wife the amount of money to be paid to her periodically under the agreement, the same legal steps may be taken to enforce his compliance as in any other breach of contract.
    II. Having obtained the writ of attachment, the plaintiff is then in the advantageous position of selling the very property that has been held for him by the sheriff while he was obtaining a judgment.

KEY (CORRECT ANSWERS)

1. C
2. D
3. C
4. C
5. D

6. D
7. A
8. C
9. B
10. B

11. E
12. A
13. C
14. D
15. E

16. C
17. D
18. C
19. B
20. C

EXAMINATION SECTION
TEST 1

DIRECTIONS: Each question or incomplete statement is followed by several suggested answers or completions. Select the one that BEST answers the question or completes the statement. *PRINT THE LETTER OF THE CORRECT ANSWER IN THE SPACE AT THE RIGHT.*

1. An indictment is a

    A. formal charge
    B. overdue payment
    C. bill of particulars relating to a dispute
    D. felony

    1.____

2. In a trial, a hostile witness is a(n) _____ witness.

    A. controversial   B. unfriendly
    C. combative   D. evasive

    2.____

3. Which of the following was an event from 1999 that may reduce the number of guns in this country?

    A. The passage of a strict gun law in Congress
    B. Gun shows were restricted by Congress
    C. The Colt Corporation restricted the sale of its guns
    D. An embargo was placed on guns coming into this country

    3.____

4. In the state, headlights should be used when visibility is equal to a minimum or less than _____ feet.

    A. 500   B. 750   C. 1,000   D. 1,250

    4.____

5. You are required to dim your headlights when an approaching vehicle is within _____ feet of your vehicle.

    A. 500   B. 400   C. 300   D. 200

    5.____

6. *Some features of the arrangement of contents in the following pages may perplex some readers.*
   The word *perplex*, as used in the above sentence, means MOST NEARLY

    A. interest   B. enlighten
    C. turnoff   D. confuse

    6.____

7. Hearsay evidence means

    A. false evidence
    B. evidence that needs to be verified
    C. it is generally not admissible in court
    D. the person testifying is unsure of its truth

    7.____

Questions 8-9.

DIRECTIONS: Questions 8 and 9 refer to the following paragraph.

The variations in report writing range from such picayune details as using A.M. or a.m. to more substantive issues as the inclusion or omission of a report summary in the first paragraph.

8. In the above paragraph, the word *picayune* means MOST NEARLY 8.____

    A. grammatic
    B. debatable
    C. trivial
    D. tendentious

9. In the above paragraph, the word *substantive* means MOST NEARLY 9.____

    A. cursory
    B. meaningless
    C. critical
    D. substantial

10. In accordance with the driver's manual issued by the state, you must report an accident when damage is _____ or more. 10.____

    A. $500   B. $1,000   C. $1,500   D. $2,000

11. It is easier to pass a heavy truck on a highway 11.____

    A. when the roadway is level
    B. when going uphill
    C. when going downhill
    D. on a concrete pavement

12. In most states, motorcyclists are required to use 12.____

    A. headlights and taillights only after sundown
    B. headlights and taillights at all times
    C. taillights only during daylight hours
    D. headlights only during daylight hours

13. DNA refers to 13.____

    A. a person who dies upon arriving at a hospital
    B. genetic material
    C. a chemical reaction
    D. a powerful drug

14. An odometer measures the _____ an automobile. 14.____

    A. speed of
    B. velocity of
    C. distance traveled by
    D. revolutions per second of the engine of

15. *Profiling has recently become a controversial issue in police work.* 15.____
    Profiling, as used in the above sentence, relates to paying special attention to

    A. a recognizable class of people
    B. people of low income

C. people who exceed the speed limits
D. the class of people who drive expensive cars

16. Most highways have a minimum speed of _____ MPH.

    A. 40 B. 35 C. 30 D. 25

17. The lowest automobile accident rate occurs in the _____ year age group.

    A. 20 to 35 B. 35 to 50 C. 50 to 65 D. 65 to 80

18. *Writing is characterized as narrative description, exposition, and argument. Exposition,* as used in the above sentence, means MOST NEARLY

    A. describing the circumstances of the situation
    B. the explanation of a piece of information
    C. explaining your conclusions
    D. giving the pros and cons of a conclusion

19. A report states that the latent prints have been sent to the laboratory. The word *latent*, as used in the above statement, means MOST NEARLY

    A. missing B. visible C. hidden D. damaged

20. After being *acquitted* in the first trial, O.J. Simpson faced a second trial. The second trial was not double jeopardy because

    A. evidence was withheld from the jury
    B. he was tried on different criminal charges
    C. the second trial was a civil trial
    D. the first trial was against the weight of the evidence

21. To *loiter* means MOST NEARLY to

    A. gather in a group of five or more
    B. create suspicion of wrongdoing while hanging around
    C. obstruct pedestrian movement
    D. linger in an aimless way

22. The minimum automobile insurance required for property damage in New York State is

    A. $3,000 B. $5,000 C. $10,000 D. $20,000

23. The maximum speed limit in a village or town is usually _____ MPH.

    A. 20 B. 25 C. 30 D. 40

24. The purpose of the *two second rule* in driving is to

    A. give you enough time to stop if there is a traffic signal ahead
    B. give you enough clearance to cut into another lane when passing a car
    C. keep enough room between your vehicle and the one ahead
    D. provide enough room when entering a highway

25. In most states, you may be arrested for driving with a blood alcohol content of _____ percent or more. 25._____

   A. .05 B. .10 C. .15 D. .20

KEY (CORRECT ANSWERS)

1. A	11. B
2. B	12. B
3. C	13. B
4. C	14. C
5. A	15. A
6. D	16. A
7. C	17. B
8. C	18. B
9. D	19. C
10. B	20. C

21. D
22. B
23. C
24. C
25. B

TEST 2

DIRECTIONS: Each question or incomplete statement is followed by several suggested answers or completions. Select the one that BEST answers the question or completes the statement. *PRINT THE LETTER OF THE CORRECT ANSWER IN THE SPACE AT THE RIGHT.*

1. A yellow sign showing two children in black indicates a school crossing. The shape of the sign is a

    A. square B. rectangle C. hexagon D. pentagon

2. Personal vehicles driven by volunteer firefighters responding to alarms are allowed to display _____ lights.

    A. blue B. green C. red D. amber

3. The color amber is closest to

    A. green B. yellow C. purple D. blue

4. Larceny in the legal sense means

    A. the unlawful taking away of another person's property without his consent
    B. overcharging another person who is making a purchase
    C. deceiving another person as to the value of an item he wishes to purchase
    D. adding a service charge to an agreed price to an item that is purchased

5. A misdemeanor in law refers to

    A. a financial dispute between two litigants
    B. a minor offense
    C. a burglary where a small amount of goods was stolen
    D. unruly behavior in public

6. An overt act means MOST NEARLY a(n)

    A. foolish act   B. act done publicly
    C. illegal act   D. outrageous act

7. A defense lawyer works for a client *pro bono*. This means he

    A. gets paid only if he wins the case
    B. gets paid a fixed fee
    C. works for free
    D. represents his client at half his usual fee

8. Corpus delicti refers to the

    A. missing person   B. murderer
    C. scene of the crime   D. dead victim

9. The shape of a stop sign is

    A. triangular   B. square
    C. six-sided   D. eight-sided

10. Service signs are _____ with white letters and symbols.

    A. blue B. green C. yellow D. red

11. Destination signs are _____ with white letters and symbols.

    A. blue B. green C. yellow D. red

12. According to the driver's manual, you are prohibited from passing if you cannot safely return to the right lane before any approaching vehicle comes within _____ feet of your car.

    A. 100 B. 150 C. 200 D. 250

13. When parking near a hydrant, you must be clear of the hydrant a minimum distance of _____ feet.

    A. 5 B. 10 C. 15 D. 20

14. When parking your vehicle between two parked vehicles, you must park a maximum of _____ inches from the curb.

    A. 12 B. 15 C. 18 D. 21

15. In order to insure approval, the framers of the Constitution agreed to add a series of amendments after approval to protect people's rights.
    The number of amendments that were added is

    A. six B. eight C. ten D. twelve

16. The amendment number that insures a person's right to bear arms is

    A. one B. two C. three D. five

17. The amendment number that prevents a person from incriminating himself is

    A. one B. three C. five D. seven

18. The right of a person to be secure in his house, and against unreasonable search is amendment number

    A. two B. four C. six D. eight

19. The right of people to assemble peaceably is amendment number

    A. one B. two C. three D. four

20. 90 kilometers per hour is equivalent to _____ MPH.

    A. 40 B. 45 C. 50 D. 55

21. A commercial driver's license is required if the vehicle being driven has a gross weight rating of equal to or more than _____ pounds.

    A. 24,000 B. 26,000 C. 28,000 D. 30,000

22. One kilogram is equivalent to _____ pounds.

    A. 2.2 B. 2.4 C. 2.6 D. 2.8

23. Failing to stop for a school bus in New York State is worth _____ points on your license. 23.____
    A. 3   B. 4   C. 5   D. 6

24. In the state, the minimum liability insurance required against the death of one person is 24.____
    A. $30,000   B. $50,000   C. $100,000   D. $150,000

25. Before a person is arrested, he is read a statement by the arresting officer. The name associated with this procedure is 25.____
    A. Megan   B. Zenger   C. Scott   D. Miranda

KEY (CORRECT ANSWERS)

1. D
2. A
3. B
4. A
5. B

6. B
7. C
8. D
9. D
10. A

11. B
12. C
13. C
14. A
15. C

16. B
17. C
18. B
19. A
20. D

21. B
22. A
23. C
24. B
25. D

TEST 3

DIRECTIONS: Each question or incomplete statement is followed by several suggested answers or completions. Select the one that BEST answers the question or completes the statement. *PRINT THE LETTER OF THE CORRECT ANSWER IN THE SPACE AT THE RIGHT.*

1. In legal terms, a deposition is

    A. a statement made by a person in open court
    B. a statement under oath, but not in open court
    C. the testimony made by a defendant under oath in open court
    D. a statement under oath that is mainly hearsay

2. In an automobile accident, first check to see if the injured person is breathing. If not, apply

    A. MPR   B. IBR   C. FHR   D. CPR

3. Hazard vehicles, such as snow plows and tow trucks, display _____ -colored lights.

    A. blue   B. green   C. amber   D. red

4. The hand signal shown at the right indicates
    A. caution because there is an obstruction ahead
    B. a right turn
    C. a left turn
    D. a stop

5. A felony is a

    A. crime only where someone is murdered
    B. major crime
    C. crime only where someone is injured
    D. crime only where major physical damage occurs

6. *Embezzlement* means MOST NEARLY

    A. deceiving   B. the hiding of funds
    C. stealing   D. investing illegally

7. The writer should be wary of using an entire paragraph for information, while necessary is not really of great importance.
   The word *wary* in the above sentence means MOST NEARLY

    A. uncertain   B. cautious
    C. certain   D. serious

8. Hearsay evidence is evidence that

    A. is usually admissible in court
    B. can be inferred from preceding evidence
    C. is based on what another person said out of court
    D. is implied in the testimony of a witness

9. *Excessive bail shall not be required* is amendment number 9.____

   A. two B. four C. six D. eight

10. The writ of habeas corpus is used to 10.____

   A. insure a defendant receives a fair trial
   B. insure a defendant's Fifth Amendment rights
   C. reduce or eliminate bail
   D. prevent a person from being detained illegally

11. The number of justices in the United States Supreme Court is 11.____

   A. 6 B. 7 C. 8 D. 9

12. The *blue wall* refers to law enforcement officers who 12.____

   A. do not publicly condemn fellow officers regardless of facts
   B. set up roadblocks
   C. support their superiors
   D. do their utmost to improve their image

13. The difference between burglary and robbery is 13.____

   A. burglary is breaking into a building to commit theft, while robbery is the use of violence in taking property from a person
   B. the money value taken in a burglary is less than $10,000, whereas in a robbery the money value taken is more than $10,000
   C. burglary takes place at night, whereas robbery takes place in the daytime
   D. burglary takes place indoors, whereas robbery takes place outdoors

14. The Federal government announced new guidelines relating to automobiles. These standards relate to 14.____

   A. automobile weight   B. gas mileage requirements
   C. car infant seats   D. bumper heights

15. General Motors was involved in a famous lawsuit relating to the Chevy Corvair based on 15.____

   A. its crashworthiness
   B. faulty design of the brake system
   C. failure of the transmissions
   D. location of the gas tanks

16. State legislatures are considering restrictions on the use of cellular phones while driving an automobile. The main argument for the restrictions is that 16.____

   A. driving with one hand is hazardous
   B. conversations on the phone are a distraction
   C. cellular phones interfere with the ignition system
   D. the driver is unlikely to hear sirens or hornblowing

17. *Much of their business involves the unpredictable and the bizarre.*
    The word *bizarre,* as used in the above statement, means MOST NEARLY 17.____

   A. weird   B. routine
   C. complicated   D. life-threatening

18. *The federal government seized 145 metric tons of cocaine coming into the United States from South America.*
    A metric ton is equal to _____ pounds.

    A. 1,800   B. 2,000   C. 2,200   D. 2,400

19. A kilogram is most nearly _____ pounds.

    A. 2.0   B. 2.2   C. 2.4   D. 2.6

20. A narcotic drug used in medicine, but less habit-forming than morphine, is

    A. cocaine   B. methadone   C. LSD   D. heroin

21. Of the following, the one that is a hazard for the large recreational vehicles is

    A. their inability to meet the emission requirements
    B. their bumper height above the ground does not match the height of the bumpers on the smaller-sized vehicles
    C. because the driver is high above the ground, his ability to see his surroundings is impaired
    D. because of the high center of gravity of the recreational vehicles, they become unstable at high speeds

22. State inspection procedures on emissions focus on

    A. hydrocarbons and CO_2
    B. CO and CO_2
    C. SO_2 and CO
    D. hydrocarbons and CO

23. *In order to bring a case before a Grand Jury, the prosecutor must present a prima facie case of guilt before the Grand Jury.*
    Prima facie in the above statement means MOST NEARLY

    A. overwhelming evidence to convict
    B. sufficient to convict unless rebutted by the defense
    C. possibly sufficient to convict by an objective jury
    D. with additional evidence would be sufficient to convict

24. The KKK was denied a permit to hold a parade in New York City. The Klan sued in court claiming a violation of their rights under the _____ Amendment.

    A. First   B. Third   C. Fifth   D. Eighth

25. In a jury trial for a felony, a jury of twelve must have

    A. a majority decision
    B. 9 members finding the defendant guilty
    C. 11 members finding the defendant guilty
    D. a unanimous finding of guilt

KEY (CORRECT ANSWERS)

1. B
2. D
3. C
4. D
5. B

6. C
7. B
8. C
9. D
10. D

11. D
12. A
13. A
14. C
15. D

16. B
17. A
18. C
19. B
20. B

21. B
22. D
23. B
24. A
25. D

TEST 4

DIRECTIONS: Each question or incomplete statement is followed by several suggested answers or completions. Select the one that BEST answers the question or completes the statement. *PRINT THE LETTER OF THE CORRECT ANSWER IN THE SPACE AT THE RIGHT.*

1. State law defines a juvenile as _____ years of age or less. 1.____

   A. 15 B. 16 C. 17 D. 18

2. A writ of habeas corpus is an order to 2.____

   A. dismiss charges against a detained person
   B. reduce the charges against a detained person
   C. have a detained person confront his accusers
   D. have a detained person brought before a court

3. A person is brought into a police station to face charges. The person brought in when interrogated refuses to tell more than his name and address. 3.____
   In the face of his silence, the proper course to be followed by the interviewer is to

   A. remind the detainee that he is guilty of obstruction of justice
   B. stop the interrogation
   C. remind the detainee that his unwillingness to cooperate will result in high bail
   D. tell the interviewee he is required to cooperate with the police

4. *The implication in most discussions on police discretion is that it is the police administrator who should undertake to spell out policies and rules.* 4.____
   In the above statement, the word *discretion* means MOST NEARLY

   A. the power to judge or act
   B. behavior
   C. competence
   D. ability to reach a conclusion

5. A nickname for amphetamine is 5.____

   A. ice B. pot C. downer D. grass

6. A nickname for cocaine is 6.____

   A. speed   B. red devils
   C. snow   D. Mary Jane

7. A nickname for marijuana is 7.____

   A. ice B. downer C. snow D. grass

8. A nickname for barbiturates is 8.____

   A. angel dust   B. quaaludes
   C. meth   D. downers

9. Of the following, the most widely used drug is

   A. LSD   B. crack   C. marijuana   D. cocaine

10. Crack is related to

    A. angel dust
    B. quaaludes
    C. LSD
    D. cocaine

11. The police department is changing the type of ammunition they use. The new bullets will have a softer head. The main reason for this change is that

    A. it will not ricochet if it hits a wall
    B. it will cause less injury to a person struck by the bullet
    C. the bullet is less expensive
    D. it will be easier to recover

12. Of the following weapons, the one that is of the semiautomatic type is the

    A. Colt revolver
    B. 45
    C. AK-47
    D. Springfield rifle

13. A *Saturday Night Special* is a

    A. semi-automatic gun
    B. small, cheaply made weapon
    C. gun used for hunting
    D. difficult gun to conceal

14. One inch is equal to _____ centimeters.

    A. 2.54   B. 2.64   C. 2.74   D. 2.84

15. A gun control bill was passed in Congress that was named after President Reagan's press secretary who was shot in an attack on the President. The name of the bill was the _____ bill.

    A. McClure
    B. Brady
    C. Volkmer
    D. Everett Koop

16. In New York City, if you are caught carrying a concealed gun for which you do not have a permit, you can be jailed for a maximum of _____ months.

    A. 3   B. 6   C. 9   D. 12

17. The Federal Firearm License Law is designed to ensure that individuals who obtain licenses have a legitimate reason for doing so and to deny guns to

    A. people who carry large amounts of money on their person
    B. people who have a criminal record
    C. senior citizens
    D. people under 22 years old

18. According to government studies, the number of guns in the United States is over _____ million.

    A. one hundred
    B. one hundred and twenty
    C. one hundred and fifty
    D. two hundred

19. According to statistics, when a woman is killed with a gun, it is LEAST likely to be by

A.	her husband	B.	a relative
C.	a stranger	D.	a friend

20. Federal law states that a person is prohibited from buying a gun who is under the age of

    A. sixteen B. eighteen
    C. twenty   D. twenty-two

21. Of the following countries in South America, the one that is the largest exporter of drugs into the United States is

    A. Columbia   B. Venezuela
    C. Chile   D. Argentina

22. Of the following, the state in the United States that allows citizens to carry concealed guns is

    A. Arizona   B. New Mexico
    C. Texas   D. Oklahoma

23. A bullet has a diameter of 9 mm. Its diameter, in inches, is MOST NEARLY _____ inch.

    A. 1/4   B. 3/8   C. 1/2   D. 5/8

24. The repeal of the amendment to the Constitution barring the manufacture and selling of whiskey occurred under the administration of President

    A. Roosevelt   B. Hoover   C. Truman   D. Coolidge

25. The shrub from which cocaine is derived is

    A. cacao   B. hemp   C. liana   D. coca

KEY (CORRECT ANSWERS)

1. D   11. A
2. D   12. C
3. B   13. B
4. A   14. A
5. A   15. B

6. C   16. D
7. D   17. B
8. D   18. D
9. C   19. C
10. D   20. B

21. A
22. C
23. B
24. A
25. D

EXAMINATION SECTION
TEST 1

DIRECTIONS: Each question or incomplete statement is followed by several suggested answers or completions. Select the one that BEST answers the question or completes the statement. *PRINT THE LETTER OF THE CORRECT ANSWER IN THE SPACE AT THE RIGHT.*

1. Officer Hayes has arrived at the scene of an automobile accident to find the two drivers arguing heatedly in the middle of the intersection, where their two cars remain entangled by their front bumpers. Traffic has backed up on all four sides of the intersection. As Officer Hayes approaches, the two drivers each begin to tell their side of the story at the same time. As they grow more agitated and begin to call each other names, one of the drivers threatens the other with physical harm.
   Officer Hayes' FIRST action should be to
   A. ask each driver to stand on an opposite corner of the intersection and wait for him to begin documenting the accident
   B. call a tow truck to clear the accident from the intersection
   C. arrest the driver who made the threat
   D. ask the drivers to pull their cars out of the intersection and off to the side of the road

2. Probably the MOST important thing a police officer can do to build and strengthen a trusting relationship with community members is to
   A. patrol the area often and conspicuously
   B. listen to them in a respectful and nonjudgmental way
   C. make sure people understand his background and qualifications
   D. establish clear, reachable goals for improving the community

3. Which of the following is NOT a factor that should influence an officer's exercise of discretion?
   A. Clear statutes and protocols
   B. Informal expectations of legislatures and the public
   C. Use of force
   D. Limited resources

4. The term for the policing style which emphasizes order maintenance is _____ style.
   A. service   B. coercive   C. watchman   D. legalistic

5. Officer Torres, a community service law enforcement officer, approaches the home of recent Vietnamese immigrants to speak to several community members gathered there. He notices several pairs of shoes on the front porch.

It is reasonable for Officer Torres too assume that
- A. the people in the home are superstitious
- B. the house must have some religious significance
- C. if he removes his own shoes before entering, it will be perceived as a sign of respect
- D. the homeowners are having their carpets cleaned

6. Ethical issues are
    - A. usually a problem only in individual behaviors
    - B. relevant to all aspects of police work
    - C. usually referred to a board or committee for decision-making
    - D. the same as legal issues

7. In using the "reflection of meaning" technique in a client interview, a social worker should do each of the following, EXCEPT
    - A. begin with a sentence stem such as "You mean…" or "Sounds like you believe…"
    - B. offer an interpretation of the client's words
    - C. add paraphrasing of longer client statements
    - D. close with a "check-out" such as, "Am I hearing you right?"

8. A police officer is speaking with a victim who is hearing-impaired. The police officer should try to do each of the following, EXCEPT
    - A. speak slowly and clearly
    - B. gradually increase the volume of his voice
    - C. face the victim squarely
    - D. reduce or eliminate any background or ambient noise

9. An officer is interviewing a witness who is a recent immigrant from China. In general, the officer should avoid
    - A. verbal tracking or requests for clarification
    - B. open-ended questions
    - C. sustained eye contact
    - D. attentive body language

10. Which of the following statements about rape is FALSE?
    - A. The use of alcohol and drugs can reduce sexual inhibitions.
    - B. Rape is a crime of violence.
    - C. Rape is a crime that can only be committed against women.
    - D. It is not a sustainable legal charge if the partner has already consented to sex in the past.

11. A person's individual code of ethics is typically determined by each of the following factors, EXCEPT
    - A. reason   B. religion   C. emotion   D. law

12. Officer Long, new to the urban precinct where he is assigned patrol, has received a pair of complaints from two customers about the owner of a local convenience store, who works the cash register on most days. According to one customer, the owner became angry and ordered her out of the store after she had asked the price of a certain item. The other customer claims that on another occasion, the owner pulled a handgun from behind the counter and trained it on him as he walked slowly out of the store with his hands up. Each of the customers has lived in the neighborhood for many years and has never before seen or heard of any strange behavior on the owner's part.
In investigating these complaints, Officer Long should suspect that
    A. the owner should be considered armed and dangerous and any entry into the store should be made with weapons drawn
    B. the cause of the problem is most likely the onset of a serious psychological disturbance
    C. the customers may have reasons to be untruthful about the convenience store owner
    D. the store owner has probably experienced a recent trauma, such as a robber attempt or a personal loss

13. Typical signs and symptoms of stress include
    I. weakened immune system   II. prolonged, vivid daydreams
    III. insomnia   IV. depression
    The CORRECT answer is:
    A. I only   B. I, III, IV   C. III, IV   D. I, II, III, IV

14. Other than solid, ethical police work, an officer's BEST defense against a lawsuit or complaint is usually
    A. detailed case records
    B. a capable advocate
    C. a vigorous counterclaim against the plaintiff
    D. the testimony of professional character witnesses

15. Assertive people
    A. avoid stating feelings, opinions, or desires
    B. appear passive, but behave aggressively
    C. state their views and needs directly
    D. appear aggressive, but behave passively

16. In the non-verbal communication process, meaning is MOST commonly provided by
    A. body language   B. touch
    C. tone of voice   D. context

17. The MOST obvious practical benefit that deviance has on a society is the
    A. advancement of the status quo
    B. vindication of new laws
    C. inducement to reach cultural goals
    D. promotion of social unity

18. What is the term for policing that focuses on providing a wider and more thorough array of social services to defeat the social problems that cause crime?
    A. Reflecting policing
    B. Order maintenance
    C. Social engineering
    D. Holistic policing

19. The term "active listening" MOSTLY refers to a person's ability to
    A. both listen and accomplish other tasks at the same time
    B. take an active role in determining which information is provided by the speaker
    C. concentrate on what is being said
    D. indicate with numerous physical cues that he/she is listening

20. Police officers in any jurisdiction are MOST likely to receive calls about
    A. threats
    B. suspicious persons
    C. petty theft or property crime
    D. disturbances, such as family arguments

21. Which of the following is NOT a physiological explanation for rape?
    A. Uncontrollable sex drive
    B. Lack of available partners
    C. Reaction to repressed desires
    D. Consequence of the natural selection process

22. Which of the following is an element of self-discipline?
    A. Establishing and reaching short-term goals
    B. Establishing and reaching long-term goals
    C. Taking an honest look at one's lifestyle and making conscious changes toward improvement
    D. Taking an honest look at one's personality and revealing traits, both good and bad, to others

23. Most of the events in a person's life are the result of
    A. chance events
    B. a sense of intuition
    C. individual choices and decisions
    D. the decisions of one's parents or other authority figures

24. Which of the following is the MOST effective way for a department to limit the discretion exercised by police officers?
    A. Open and flexible departmental directives
    B. Close supervision by departmental management
    C. Broadening role definitions for officers
    D. Statutory protection from civil liability lawsuits

25. Police officers who demonstrate critical thinking skills are also more likely to demonstrate each of the following, EXCEPT
    A. the ability to empathize
    B. the tendency to criticize
    C. self-awareness
    D. reflective thinking

    25.____

KEY (CORRECT ANSWERS)

1.	A		11.	D
2.	B		12.	D
3.	A		13.	B
4.	C		14.	A
5.	C		15.	C
6.	B		16.	A
7.	B		17.	D
8.	B		18.	D
9.	C		19.	C
10.	D		20.	D

21.	C
22.	C
23.	C
24.	B
25.	B

TEST 2

DIRECTIONS: Each question or incomplete statement is followed by several suggested answers or completions. Select the one that BEST answers the question or completes the statement. *PRINT THE LETTER OF THE CORRECT ANSWER IN THE SPACE AT THE RIGHT.*

1. Officer Park responds to a domestic disturbance call to find a mother and her two young children huddled together in the living room, all of them crying. The mother explains that her husband is no longer there; he flew into a fit of rage and then stormed out to join his friends for a night of drinking.
   Officer Park's FIRST action would MOST likely be to
   A. determine the location of the husband
   B. contact the appropriate social services agency to arrange a consultation
   C. try to calm the family down and ask the mother to explain what happened
   D. refer the mother to a local battered-spouse shelter

   1.____

2. Most commonly, the reason for crimes involving stranger violence is
   A. anger   B. retaliation   C. hate   D. robbery

   2.____

3. For a police officer, "burst stress" is MOST likely to be caused by
   A. a shootout   B. financial troubles
   C. departmental politics   D. substance abuse

   3.____

4. The MOST significant factor in whether a person achieves success in his/her personal life, school, and career is
   A. intelligence   B. a positive attitude
   C. existing financial resources   D. innate ability

   4.____

5. Typically, a professional code of ethics
   A. embodies a broad picture of expected moral conduct
   B. is voluntary
   C. provides specific guidance for performance in situations
   D. are decided by objective ethicists outside of the profession

   5.____

6. Components recognized by contemporary society as elements of sexual harassment include
   I. abuse of power   II. immature behavior
   III. sexual desire   IV. hormonal imbalance
   The CORRECT answer is:
   A. I only   B. I, III   C. II, III   D. I, II, III, IV

   6.____

7. The phrase "substance abuse" is typically defined as
   A. an addiction to an illegal substance
   B. the continued use of a psychoactive substance even after it creates problems in a person's life
   C. the overuse of an illegal substance
   D. a situation in which a person craves a drug and organizes his or her life around obtaining it

   7.____

8. The humanist perspective of behavior holds that people who commit crimes or otherwise act badly are
    A. willfully disregarding societal norms
    B. reacting to the deprivation of basic needs
    C. suffering from a psychological illness
    D. experiencing a moral lapse

8.____

9. Which of the following is NOT involved in the process of empathic listening?
    A. Actually hearing exactly what the other person is saying
    B. Searching for the "hidden meanings" behind statements
    C. Listening without judgment
    D. Communicating that you're hearing what the other person is saying, both verbally and nonverbally

9.____

10. Which of the following is NOT a component in developing a stress-resistant lifestyle?
    A. Finding leisure time
    B. Eating nutritious foods
    C. Getting enough sleep
    D. Seeking financial independence

10.____

11. Which of the following was NOT a factor that led to the expansion of a community policing model?
    A. Information obtained at a crime scene during a preliminary investigation was the most important factor determining the probability of an arrest.
    B. Police response times typically had little to do with the probability of making an arrest.
    C. Traditional "preventive patrols" generally failed to reduce crime.
    D. People who knew police officers personally often tried to take advantage of them.

11.____

12. Most of the correspondence in a pyramid scheme that has defrauded several elderly victims has been traced to a post office box in a rural area.
    Probably the simplest and most efficient way of arresting the suspect(s) in this case would be to
    A. use an elderly man as a "victim" to lure the suspects into an attempt to defraud him
    B. address a letter to the post office box asking the user to come in for questioning
    C. check Postal Service records to see who is leasing the post office box
    D. physically observe the post office box for a while, to see who is using it

12.____

13. The process of hiring a police officer typically involves each of the following, EXCEPT
    A. technical preparation
    B. medical examination
    C. background checks
    D. physical ability test

13.____

14. The MOST common form of rape is _____ rape.
    A. stranger
    B. acquaintance
    C. sadistic
    D. spousal

14.____

15. Officer Stevens and his partner respond to a domestic disturbance call involving a father and his teenage daughter. As the officers arrive at their home, the two are still arguing heatedly, but when the officers enter, the daughter retreats to the kitchen, where she continues crying. The father explains that his wife, the daughter's mother, died last year, and the daughter's behavior and school performance have suffered as a result. The father is afraid that the daughter is falling in with the wrong crowd, and may be getting involved with drugs. He is afraid for her and doesn't know what to do.
Within the scope of his police role, the MOST appropriate action for Officer Stevens to take in this case would be to
    A. warn both the father and the daughter of the potential consequences of conviction on a charge of disturbing the peace
    B. refer the father and the daughter to a social services or counseling agency
    C. inform the daughter of the drug statutes that may apply in her case as a way to influence her choices
    D. question the daughter about her feelings surrounding the death of her mother

15.____

16. During an interview, a suspect confesses to the rape of a co-worker that occurred in the office after the rest of the employees had left for the day. The suspect says he was tormented by the seductive behavior of the co-worker until he could no longer stand it. He was himself a victim, he says.
In this case, the suspect is making use of the psychological defense mechanism known as
    A. projection   B. regression   C. denial   D. sublimation

16.____

17. Which of the following is NOT a good stress-reduction strategy?
    A. Spend some time each day doing absolutely nothing
    B. Become more assertive
    C. Develop a hobby
    D. Have a sense of humor

17.____

18. The term for the policing style which emphasizes problem-solving is _____ style.
    A. watchman   B. order maintenance
    C. service   D. legalistic

18.____

19. According to current rules and statutes, any employer
    A. may inquire as to a job applicant's age or date of birth
    B. may keep on file information regarding an employee's race, color, religion, sex, or national origin
    C. may refuse employment to someone without a car
    D. must give a woman who has taken time off for maternity leave her same job and salary when she is read to return to work

19.____

20. During a conversation with the mother of a teenage boy who has been arrested twice for shoplifting, an officer attempts to be an active listener as the mother explains why she thinks the boy is having so much trouble.
Being an active listener includes each of the following strategies, EXCEPT
   A. putting the speaker at ease
   B. interrupting with questions to clarify meaning
   C. summarizing the speaker's major ideas and feelings
   D. withholding criticism

21. Which of the following is NOT a characteristic of the typical poverty-class family?
   A. Female-headed, single-parent families
   B. Unwed parents
   C. Isolated from neighbors and relatives
   D. High divorce rates

22. When speaking with community members about improving the quality of life in the neighborhood, an officer should look for signs of social desirability bias among the people with whom he's talking.
Social desirability bias often causes people to
   A. judge other people based on their social role rather than inner character
   B. attribute their successes to skill, while blaming external factors for failures
   C. modify their interactions or behaviors based on what they think is acceptable to others
   D. contend for leadership positions

23. For a number of reasons, Officer Stone thinks a fellow officer might have a drinking problem, and decides to talk to her about it. The officer says she doesn't have a drinking problem; she doesn't even take a drink until after it gets dark.
Her answer indicates that she
   A. doesn't have a drinking problem
   B. is probably a social drinker
   C. drinks more during the winter months
   D. is in denial

24. Factors which shape the police role include each of the following, EXCEPT
   A. individual goals   B. role expectations
   C. role acquisition   D. multiple-role phenomenon

25. "Deviance" is a social term denoting
   A. any violation of norms
   B. any serious violation of norms
   C. a type of nonconforming behavior recognizable in all cultures
   D. a specific set of crime statistics

KEY (CORRECT ANSWERS)

1.	C		11.	D
2.	D		12.	D
3.	A		13.	A
4.	B		14.	B
5.	A		15.	B
6.	A		16.	A
7.	B		17.	A
8.	B		18.	C
9.	B		19.	B
10.	D		20.	B

21. C
22. C
23. D
24. A
25. A

EXAMINATION SECTION
TEST 1

DIRECTIONS: Each question or incomplete statement is followed by several suggested answers or completions. Select the one that BEST answers the question or completes the statement. *PRINT THE LETTER OF THE CORRECT ANSWER IN THE SPACE AT THE RIGHT.*

1. The delivery of an arrested person to his sureties, upon their giving security for his appearance at the time and place designated to submit to the jurisdiction and judgment of the court, is known as
   A. bail
   B. habeas corpus
   C. parole
   D. probation

   1.____

2. Jones was charged with the murder of Smith. Brown, Jones' landlord, testified at the trial that Jones had in his home a well-equipped laboratory which contained all the necessary chemical for producing the poison which an autopsy showed caused Smith's death.
   Brown's testimony constitutes what is called _____ evidence.
   A. corroborative   B. opinion   C. hearsay   D. circumstantial

   2.____

3. In addressing a class of recruits, a police lieutenant remarked: "Carelessness and failure are twins."
   The one of the following that MOST NEARLY expresses his meaning is
   A. negligence seldom accompanies success
   B. incomplete work is careless work
   C. conscientious work is never attended by failure
   D. a conscientious person never makes mistakes

   3.____

4. In taking a statement from a person who has been shot by an assailant and is not expected to live, police are instructed to ask the person: "Do you believe you are about to die?"
   Of the following, the MOST probable reason for this question is
   A. the theory that a person about to die will tell the truth
   B. to determine if the victim is conscious and capable of making a statement
   C. to put the victim mentally at ease and more willing to talk
   D. that the statement could not be used in court if his mind was distraught by the fear of impending death

   4.____

5. If, while you are on duty at a busy intersection, a pedestrian asks you for directions to a particular place, the BEST course of conduct is to
   A. ignore the question and continue directing operations
   B. tell the pedestrian to ask a patrolman on foot patrol
   C. answer the question in a brief, courteous manner
   D. leave your post only long enough to give clear and adequate directions

   5.____

6. In lecturing on the law of arrest, a lieutenant remarked: "To go beyond is as bad as to fall short."
 The one of the following which MOST NEARLY expresses his meaning is
 A. never undertake the impossible   B. extremes are not desirable
 C. look before you leap   D. too much success is dangerous

6.____

7. Suppose you are an officer assigned to a patrol precinct. While you are in the vicinity of a school, your attention is called to a man who is selling small packages to school children. You are told that this man distributes similar packages to these same children daily and that he is suspected of dealing in narcotics.
 Of the following, the BEST action for you to take is to
 A. pretend to be an addict and attempt to purchase narcotics from him
 B. observe the man's action yourself for several days in order to obtain grounds for arrest
 C. stop and question one or more of the children after they have transacted business with the man
 D. stop and question the man as he leaves the children

7.____

8. In the event of a poison gas attack, civil defense authorities advise civilians to _____ door and windows and go to _____.
 A. open; upper floors   B. close; upper floors
 C. open; the basement   D. close; the basement

8.____

9. The procedure whereby a defendant is brought before a magistrate, informed of the charge against him, and asked how he pleads thereto, is called
 A. arraignment   B. indictment   C. presentment   D. inquisition

9.____

10. A written accusation of a crime presented by a grand jury is called a(n)
 A. commitment   B. arraignment   C. indictment   D. demurrer

10.____

11. The one of the following statements made by a prisoner that is correctly called an alibi is:
 A. "He struck me first."
 B. "I didn't intend to hurt him."
 C. "I was miles away from there at the time."
 D. "I don't remember what happened."

11.____

12. A person who, after the commission of a crime, conceals the defender with the intent that the latter may escape from arrest and trial, is called a(n)
 A. accessory   B. accomplice   C. confederate   D. associate

12.____

13. A sworn statement of fact is called a(n)
 A. affidavit   B. oath
 C. acknowledgment   D. subpoena

13.____

14. The right of trial by jury in the courts of the state is PRIMARILY safeguarded by a provision of
    A. the United States Constitution B. the constitution of the state
    C. a state statute D. a Federal statute

15. The task of protecting the President and his family is entrusted PRIMARILY to the
    A. Federal Bureau of Investigation
    B. United States Secret Service
    C. Central Intelligence Agency
    D. District of Columbia Police Department

16. The coordinating organization for the various Federal agencies engaged in intelligence activities is the
    A. Federal Bureau of Investigation B. Federal Security Agency
    C. Mutual Security Agency D. Central Intelligence Agency

17. A drug addict whose arm shows many scars from the injection of a hypodermic needle is MOST apt to be addicted to
    A. heroin B. cocaine C. opium D. marijuana

18. All of the following drugs are derived from opium EXCEPT
    A. cocaine B. heroin C. morphine D. codeine

19. In addition to cases of submersion, artificial respiration is a recommended first aid procedure for
    A. sunstroke B. chemical poisoning
    C. electric shock D. apoplexy

20. An injury to a muscle or tendon brought about by severe exertion and resulting in pain and stiffness is called a
    A. strain B. sprain C. bruise D. fracture

21. Of the following kinds of wounds, the one in which there is the LEAST danger of infection is a(n) _____ wound.
    A. abrasive B. punctured C. lacerated D. incised

22. When a person is found injured on the street, it is generally advisable, pending arrival of a physician, to help prevent fainting or shock by keeping the patient
    A. in a sitting position B. lying down with the head level
    C. lying down with the head raised D. standing on his feet

23. When an injured person appears to be suffering from shock, of the following, it is MOST essential to
    A. loosen his clothing B. keep him warm
    C. administer a stimulant D. place him in a prone position

24. In the sentence, "Malice was immanent in all his remarks," the word "immanent" means MOST NEARLY
    A. elevated   B. inherent   C. threatening   D. foreign

25. In the sentence, "The extant copies of the document were found in the safe," the word "extant" means MOST NEARLY
    A. existing   B. original   C. forged   D. duplicate

26. In the sentence, "The recruit was more complaisant after the captain spoke to him," the word "complaisant" means MOST NEARLY
    A. calm   B. affable   C. irritable   D. confident

27. In the sentence, "The man was captured under highly creditable circumstances," the word "creditable" means MOST NEARLY
    A. doubtful   B. believable   C. praiseworthy   D. unexpected

28. In the sentence, "His superior officers were more sagacious than he," the word "sagacious" means MOST NEARLY
    A. shrewd   B. obtuse   C. absurd   D. verbose

29. In the sentence, "He spoke with impunity," the word "impunity" means MOST NEARLY
    A. rashness   B. caution   C. without fear   D. immunity

30. In the sentence, "The new patrolman displayed unusual temerity during the emergency," the word "temerity" means MOST NEARLY
    A. fear   B. rashness   C. calmness   D. anxiety

31. In the sentence, "The portions of food were parsimoniously served," the word "parsimoniously" means MOST NEARLY
    A. stingily   B. piously   C. elaborately   D. generously

32. In the sentence, "Generally the speaker's remarks were sententious," the word "sententious" means MOST NEARLY
    A. verbose   B. witty
    C. argumentative   D. pithy

33. In the sentence, "The prisoner was fractious when brought to the station house," the word "fractious" means MOST NEARLY
    A. penitent   B. talkative   C. irascible   D. broken-hearted

34. In the sentence, "The judge was implacable when the attorney pleaded for leniency," the word "implacable" means MOST NEARLY
    A. inexorable   B. disinterested
    C. inattentive   D. indifferent

35. In the sentence, "The court ordered the mendacious statements stricken from the record," the word "mendacious" means MOST NEARLY
    A. begging   B. lying   C. threatening   D. lengthy

36. In the sentence, "The district attorney spoke in a strident voice," the word "strident" means MOST NEARLY
    A. loud
    B. harsh-sounding
    C. sing-song
    D. low

37. In the sentence, "The speaker had a predilection for long sentences," the word "predilection" means MOST NEARLY
    A. aversion
    B. talent
    C. propensity
    D. diffidence

38. In the sentence, "The candidate wants to file his application for preference before it is too late," the word "before" is used as a(n)
    A. preposition
    B. subordinating conjunction
    C. pronoun
    D. adverb

39. The one of the following sentences which is grammatically PREFERABLE to the others is:
    A. Our engineers will go over your blueprints so that you may have no problems in construction.
    B. For a long time he had been arguing that we, not he, are to blame for the confusion.
    C. I worked on this automobile for two hours and still cannot find out what is wrong with it.
    D. Accustomed to all kinds of hardships, fatigue seldom bothers veteran policemen.

40. The plural of
    A. turkey is turkies
    B. cargo is cargoes
    C. bankruptcy is bankruptcys
    D. son-in-law is son-in-laws

41. The abbreviation "viz." means MOST NEARLY
    A. namely
    B. for example
    C. the following
    D. see

42. In the sentence, "A man in a light-grey suit waited thirty-five minutes in the ante-room for the all-important document," the word IMPROPERLY hyphenated is
    A. light-grey
    B. thirty-five
    C. ante-room
    D. all-important

43. The MOST accurate of the following sentences is:
    A. The commissioner, as well as his deputy and various bureau heads, were present.
    B. A new organization of employers and employees have been formed.
    C. One or the other of these men have been selected.
    D. The number of pages in the book is enough to discourage a reader.

44. The MOST accurate of the following sentences is:
    A. Between you and me, I think he is the better man.
    B. He was believed to be me.
    C. Is it us that you wish to see?
    D. The winners are him and her.

45. In the sentence, "The committee favored submiting the amendment to the electorate," the MISSPELLED word is
    A. committee B. submiting C. amendment D. electorate

46. In the sentence, "He maliciously demurred to an ajournment of the proceedings," the MISSPELLED word is
    A. maliciously B. demurred C. ajournment D. proceedings

47. In the sentence, "His innocence at that time is irrelevent in view of his more recent villainous demeanor," the MISSPELLED word is
    A. innocence B. irrelevent C. villainous D. demeanor

48. In the sentence, "The mischievous boys aggrevated the annoyance of their neighbor," the MISSPELLED word is
    A. mischievous B. aggrevated C. annoyance D. neighbor

49. In the sentence, "While his persiverance was commendable, his judgment was debatable, the MISSPELLED word is
    A. persiverance   B. commendable
    C. judgment   D. debatable

50. In the sentence, "He was hoping the appeal would facilitate his aquittal," the MISSPELLED word is
    A. hoping B. appeal C. facilitate D. aquittal

51. In the sentence, "It would be preferable for them to persue separate courses," the MISSPELLED word is
    A. preferable B. persue C. separate D. courses

52. In the sentence, "The litigant was complimented on his persistance and achievement," the MISSPELLED word is
    A. litigant   B. complimented
    C. persistance   D. achievement

53. In the sentence, "Ocassionally there are discrepancies in the descriptions of miscellaneous items," the MISSPELLED word is
    A. ocassionally   B. discrepancies
    C. descriptions   D. miscellaneous

54. In the sentence, "The councilmanic seargent-at-arms enforced the prohibition," the MISSPELLED word is
    A. councilmanic   B. seargent-at-arms
    C. enforced   D. prohibition

55. In the sentence, "The teacher had an ingenious device for mantaining attendance," the MISSPELLED word is
    A. ingenious B. device C. mantaining D. attendance

Questions 56-63.

DIRECTIONS: Questions 56 through 63 are to be answered on the basis of the following excerpt from a recorded annual report of the police department. This material should be read first and then referred to in answering these questions, which are to be answered SOLELY on the basis of the material herein contained.

LEGAL BUREAU

One of the more important functions of this bureau is to analyze and furnish the department with pertinent information concerning Federal and State statutes and Local Laws which affect the department, law enforcement or crime prevention. In addition, all measures introduced in the State Legislature and the City Council which may affect this department are carefully reviewed by members of the Legal Bureau and, where necessary, opinions and recommendations thereon are prepared.

Another important function of this office is the prosecution of cases in the Magistrate's Courts. This is accomplished by assignment of attorneys who are members of the Legal Bureau to appear in those cases which are deemed to raise issues of importance to the department or questions of law which require technical presentation to facilitate proper determination; and also in those cases where request is made for such appearances by a magistrate, some other official of the city, or a member of the force. Attorneys are regularly assigned to prosecute all cases in the Women's Court.

Proposed legislation was prepared and sponsored for introduction in the State Legislature and, at this writing, one of these proposals has already been enacted into law and five others are presently on the Governor's desk awaiting executive action. The new law prohibits the sale or possession of a hypodermic syringe or needle by an unauthorized person. The bureau's proposals awaiting executive action pertain to an amendment to the Code of Criminal Procedure prohibiting desk officers from taking bail in gambling cases or in cases mentioned in Section 552, Code of Criminal Procedure; including confidence men and swindlers as jostlers in the Penal Law; prohibiting the sale of switchblade knives of any size to children under 16 and bills extending the licensing period of gunsmiths.

The Legal Bureau has regularly cooperated with the Corporation Counsel and the District Attorneys in respect to matters affecting this department, and has continued to advise and represent the Police Athletic League, the Police Sports Association, the Police Relief Fund, and the Police Pension Fund.

The following is a statistical report of the activities of the bureau during the current year as compared with the previous year:

	Current Year	Previous Year
Memoranda of law prepared	68	83
Legal matters forwarded to corporation counsel	122	144
Letters requesting legal information	756	807
Letters requesting departmental records	139	111
Matters for publication	17	26
Court appearances of members of bureau	4,678	4,621
Conferences	94	103
Lectures at Police Academy	30	33
Reports on proposed legislation	194	255
Deciphering of codes	79	27
Expert testimony	31	16
Notices to court witnesses	55	81
Briefs prepared	22	18
Court papers prepared	258	--

56. One of the functions of the Legal Bureau is to
    A. review and make recommendations on proposed Federal laws affecting law enforcement
    B. prepare opinions on all measures introduced in the State Legislature and the City Council
    C. furnish the Police Department with pertinent information concerning all new Federal and State laws
    D. analyze all laws affecting the work of the Police Department

57. The one of the following that is NOT a function of the Legal Bureau is
    A. law enforcement and crime prevention
    B. prosecution of all cases in Women's Court
    C. advise and represent the Police Sports Association
    D. lecturing at the Police Academy

58. Members of the Legal Bureau frequently appear in Magistrate's Court for the purpose of
    A. defending members of the Police Force
    B. raising issues of importance to the Police Department
    C. prosecuting all offenders arrested by members of the Force
    D. facilitating proper determination of questions of law requiring technical presentation

59. The Legal Bureau sponsored a bill that would
    A. extend the licenses of gunsmiths
    B. prohibit the sale of switchblade knives to children of any size
    C. place confidence men and swindlers in the same category as jostlers in the Penal Law
    D. prohibit desk officers from admitting gamblers, confidence men, and swindlers to bail

60. From the report, it is NOT reasonable to infer that 60.____
    A. fewer bills affecting the Police Department were introduced in the current year
    B. the preparation of court papers was a new activity assumed in the current year
    C. the Code of Criminal Procedure authorizes desk officers to accept bail in certain cases
    D. the penalty for jostling and swindling is the same

61. According to the statistical report, the activity showing the GREATEST percentage of decrease in the current year as compared to the previous year was 61.____
    A. matters for publication   B. reports on proposed legislation
    C. notices to court witnesses   D. memoranda of law prepared

62. According to the statistical report, the activity showing the GREATEST percentage of increase in the current year as compare with the previous year was 62.____
    A. court appearances of members of the bureau
    B. giving expert testimony
    C. deciphering of codes
    D. letters requesting departmental records

63. According to the report, the percentage of bills prepared and sponsored by the Legal Bureau which were passed by the State Legislature and sent to the Governor for approval was APPROXIMATELY 63.____
    A. 3.1%
    B. 2.6%
    C. .5%
    D. not capable of determination from the data given

64. A squad of officers assigned to enforce a new parking regulation in a particular area issued tag summonses on a particular day as follows: four officers issued 16 summonses each; three issued 19 each; one issued 22; seven issued 25 each; eleven issued 28 each; ten issued 30 each; two issued 36 each; one issued 41; and three issued 45 each.
    The average number of summonses issued by a member of this squad was MOST NEARLY 64.____
    A. 6.2   B. 17.2   C. 21.0   D. 27.9

65. A water storage tank is 75 feet long and 30 feet wide and has a depth of 6½ feet. Each cubic foot of the tank holds 9½ gallons.
    The TOTAL capacity of the tank is _____ gallons. 65.____
    A. 73,125½   B. 131,625   C. 138,937½   D. 146,250

66. The price of admission to a PAL entertainment were $2.50 each for adults and $1.00 for children; the turnstile at the entrance showed that 358 persons entered and the gate receipts were $626.50.
The number of children who attended was
   A. 170   B. 175   C. 179   D. 183

67. A patrol car travels six times as fast as a bicycle.
If the patrol car goes 168 miles in two hours less time than the bicycle requires to go 42 miles, their respective rates of speed are _____ miles per hour.
   A. 36 and 6   B. 42 and 7   C. 63 and 10½   D. 126 and 21

68. The radiator of an automobile already contains six quarts of a 10% solution of alcohol.
In order to make a mixture of 20% alcohol, it will be necessary to add _____ quarts of alcohol.
   A. ¾   B. 1¾   C. 2½   D. 3

69. A man received an inheritance of $80,000 and wanted to invest it so that it would produce an annual income sufficient to pay his rent of $400 a month. In order to do this, he will have to receive interest or dividends at the rate of _____% per annum.
   A. 3   B. 4   C. 5¾   D. 6

70. If the price of a bus ticket varies *directly* as the mileage involved, and a ticket to travel 135 miles costs $29.70, a ticket for a 30-mile trip will cost
   A. $15.20   B. $13.40   C. $6.60   D. $2.20

71. A man owed a debt of $5,800. After a first payment of $100, he agreed to pay the balance by monthly payments in which each payment after this first would be $20 more than that of the preceding month.
If no interest charge is made, he will have to make, including the first payment, a total of _____ monthly payments.
   A. 16   B. 20   C. 24   D. 28

72. The written test of a civil service examination has a weight of 30, the oral test a weight of 20, experience a weight of 20, and the physical test a weight of 30. A candidate received ratings of 76 on the written test, 84 on the oral, and 80 for experience.
In order to attain an average of 85 on the examination, his rating on the physical test must be
   A. 86   B. 90   C. 94   D. 98

73. A family has an income of $3,200 per month. It spends 22% of this amount for rent, 36% for food, 16% for clothing, and 12% for additional household expenses. After meeting these expenses, 50% of the balance is deposited in the bank.
The amount deposited monthly is
   A. $224.00   B. $366.00   C. $448.00   D. $520.00

11 (#1)

74. Upon retirement last July, an officer bought a farm of 64 acres for $18,000 per acre. He made a down payment of $612,000 and agreed to pay the balance in installments of $7,500 a month commencing on August 1, 2022.
Disregarding interest, he will make his LAST payment in
    A. July 2028
    B. August 2030
    C. January 2032
    D. April 2035

75. 40% of those who commit a particular crime are subsequently arrested and convicted. 75% of those committed receive sentences of 10 years or more. Assuming that those arrested for the first time serve less than 10 years, the percentage of those committing this crime who receive sentences of ten years or more is MOST NEARLY
    A. 20%
    B. 30%
    C. 40%
    D. 50%

KEY (CORRECT ANSWERS)

1.	A	21.	D	41.	A	61.	A
2.	D	22.	B	42.	C	62.	C
3.	A	23.	B	43.	D	63.	D
4.	A	24.	B	44.	A	64.	D
5.	C	25.	A	45.	B	65.	C
6.	B	26.	B	46.	C	66.	C
7.	C	27.	C	47.	C	67.	B
8.	B	28.	A	48.	B	68.	A
9.	A	29.	D	49.	A	69.	D
10.	C	30.	B	50.	D	70.	C
11.	C	31.	A	51.	B	71.	B
12.	A	32.	D	52.	C	72.	D
13.	A	33.	C	53.	A	73.	A
14.	B	34.	A	54.	B	74.	A
15.	B	35.	B	55.	C	75.	B
16.	D	36.	B	56.	D		
17.	A	37.	C	57.	A		
18.	A	38.	B	58.	D		
19.	C	39.	A	59.	C		
20.	A	40.	B	60.	D		

EXAMINATION SECTION
TEST 1

DIRECTIONS: Each question or incomplete statement is followed by several suggested answers or completions. Select the one that BEST answers the question or completes the statement. *PRINT THE LETTER OF THE CORRECT ANSWER IN THE SPACE AT THE RIGHT.*

1. The basic purpose of patrol is to create a public impression of police presence everywhere so that potential offenders will think there is no opportunity for successful misconduct.
   In the assignment of police personnel, the type of police activity that MOST NEARLY realizes this purpose is
   A. traffic summons duty
   B. traffic duty
   C. patrol of all licensed premises
   D. patrol by the detective force
   E. radio motor patrol

   1._____

2. A patrolman, who is asked by a civilian about a legal matter, directs him to the appropriate court.
   Of the following information given by the patrolman, the item which is LEAST likely to be useful to the civilian is
   A. hours during which the court is in session
   B. location of the court
   C. name of the Magistrate sitting in this court
   D. location of the complaint clerk within the court building
   E. transportation directions necessary to get to the court

   2._____

3. An officer discovers two teenaged gangs, numbering about 50 boys, engaged in a free-for-all fight.
   The BEST immediate course for the officer to adopt is to
   A. call the station house for reinforcements
   B. fire over the heads of the boys and order them to disperse
   C. arrest the ringleaders
   D. call upon adult bystanders to assist him in restoring order
   E. attempt to stop the fight by using his club

   3._____

4. A radio motor patrol team arrives on the scene a few minutes after a pedestrian has been killed on a busy street by a hit-and-run driver.
   After obtaining a description of the car, the FIRST action the officer should take is to
   A. radio a description of the fleeing car to precinct headquarters
   B. try to overtake the fleeing car
   C. obtain complete statements from everyone at the scene
   D. call for an ambulance
   E. inspect the site of the accident for clues

   4._____

5. A police officer is approached by an obviously upset woman who reports that her husband is missing.
   The FIRST thing the officer should do is to
   A. check with the hospitals and the police station
   B. tell the woman to wait a few hours and call the police station if her husband has not returned by then
   C. obtain a description of the missing man so that an alarm can be broadcast
   D. ask the woman why she thinks her husband is missing
   E. make certain that the woman lives in his precinct

6. A violin is reported as missing from the home of Mrs. Brown.
   It would be LEAST important to the police, before making a routine check of pawnshops, to know that this violin
   A. is of a certain unusual shade of red
   B. has dimensions which are different from those of most violins
   C. has a well-known manufacturer's label stamped inside the violin
   D. has a hidden number given to the police by the owner
   E. has one tuning key with a chip mark on it in the shape of a triangle

7. In making his rounds, an officer should following the same route and schedule each time.
   The suggested procedure is
   A. *good*; a fixed routine enables the officer to proceed methodically and systematically
   B. *poor*; criminals can avoid observation by studying the officer's routine
   C. *good*; without a fixed routine, an officer may overlook some of his many duties
   D. *poor*; a fixed routine reduces an officer's alertness and initiative
   E. *good*; residents in the area covered will have more confidence in police efficiency

8. Police officers should call for ambulances to transport injured people to the hospital rather than use patrol cars for this purpose.
   Of the following, the MOST valid reason for this policy is that
   A. there is less danger of aggravating injuries
   B. patrol cars cannot be spared from police duty
   C. patrol cars are usually not equipped for giving emergency first aid
   D. medical assistance reaches the injured person sooner
   E. responsibility for treating injured people lies with the Department of Hospitals

9. A businessman requests advice concerning good practice in the use of a safe in his business office.
   The one of the following points which should be stressed MOST in the use of safes is that
   A. a safe should not be placed where it can be seen from the street
   B. the combination should be written down and carefully hidden in the office

C. a safe located in a dark place is more tempting to a burglar than one which is located in a well-lighted place
D. factors of size and weight alone determine the protection offered by a safe
E. the names of the manufacturer and the owner should be painted on the front of the safe

10. During a quarrel on a crowded city street, one man stabs another and flees. An officer arriving at the scene a short time later finds the victim unconscious, calls for an ambulance, and orders the crowd to leave.
His action was
    A. *bad*; there may have witnesses to the assault among the crowd
    B. *good*; it is proper first aid procedure to give an injured person room and air
    C. *bad*; the assailant is probably among the crowd
    D. *good*; a crowd may destroy needed evidence
    E. *bad*; it is poor public relations for the police to order people about needlessly

10.____

11. An officer walking his post at 3 A.M. notices heavy smoke coming out of a top floor window of a large apartment house.
Of the following, the action he should take FIRST is to
    A. make certain that there really is a fire
    B. enter the building and warn all the occupants of the apartment house
    C. attempt to extinguish the fire before it gets out of control
    D. call the Fire Department
    E. call precinct headquarters for Fire Department help

11.____

12. Two rival youth gangs have been involved in several minor classes. The youth officer working in their area believes that a serious clash will occur if steps are not taken to prevent it.
Of the following, the LEAST desirable action for the officer to take in his effort to head of trouble is to
    A. arrest the leaders of both groups as a warning
    B. warn the parents of the dangerous situation
    C. obtain the cooperation of religious and civic leaders in the community
    D. alert all social agencies working in that neighborhood
    E. report the situation to his superior

12.____

13. Police officers are instructed to pay particular attention to anyone apparently making repairs on an auto parked on a street.
The MOST important reason for this rule is that
    A. the auto may be parked illegally
    B. the person making the repairs may be obstructing traffic
    C. working on autos is prohibited on certain streets
    D. many people injure themselves while working on autos
    E. the person making the repairs may be stealing the auto

13.____

14. After making an arrest of a criminal, the officer is LEAST likely to request some kind of transportation if the
    A. prisoner is apparently a violent mental patient
    B. distance to be traveled is considerable
    C. prisoner is injured
    D. prisoner is in an alcoholic stupor
    E. prisoner talks of escaping

15. The Police Department, in an effort to prevent losses due to worthless checks, suggests to merchants that they place near the cash register a card stating that the merchant reserves the right to require positive identification and fingerprint from all persons who cash checks.
    This procedure is
    A. *poor*; the merchant's regular customers may be offended by compulsory fingerprinting
    B. *poor*; the taking of fingerprints would not deter the professional criminal
    C. *good*; the police criminal files may be enlarged by the addition of all fingerprints taken
    D. *poor*; this system could not work unless the fingerprinting was made mandatory
    E. *good*; the card might serve to discourage persons from attempting to cash worthless checks

16. A factory manager asks an officer to escort his payroll clerk to and from the local bank when payroll money is withdrawn. The officer knows that it is against departmental policy to provide payroll escort service.
    The officer should
    A. refuse and explain why he cannot do what is requested
    B. refer the manager to his precinct commander
    C. tell the manager that police officers have more important tasks
    D. advise the manager that he will provide this service if other duties do not interfere
    E. suggest that paychecks be issued to employees

17. A motorist who has been stopped by a motorcycle police officer for speeding acts rudely. He hints about his personal connections with high officials in the city government and demands the officer's name and shield number.
    The officer should
    A. arrest the motorist for threatening an officer in the performance of his duty
    B. give his name and shield number without comment
    C. ignore the question since his name and shield number will be on the summons he is about to issue
    D. give his name and shield number but add to the charges against the motorist
    E. ask the motorist why he wants the information and give it only if the answer is satisfactory

18. Tire skidmarks provide valuable information to policemen investigating automobile accidents.
    The MOST important information obtained from this source is the
    A. condition of the road at the time of the accident
    B. effectiveness of the automobile's brakes
    C. condition of the tires
    D. point at which the driver first saw the danger
    E. speed of the automobile at the time of the accident

19. An officer observes several youths in the act of looting a peanut-vending machine. The youths flee in several directions as he approaches, ignoring his order to halt. The officer then shoots at them, and they halt and are captured
    The officer's action was
    A. *right*; it was the most effective way of capturing the criminals
    B. *wrong*; extreme measures should not be taken in apprehending petty offenders
    C. *right*; provided that there was no danger of shooting innocent bystanders
    D. *wrong*; this is usually ineffective when more than one offender is involved
    E. *right*; it is particularly important to teach juvenile delinquents respect for the law

20. Before permitting automobiles involved in an accident to depart, an officer should take certain measures.
    Of the following, it is LEAST important that the officer make certain that
    A. both drivers are properly licensed
    B. the automobiles are in safe operating condition
    C. the drivers have exchanged names and license numbers
    D. the drivers are physically fit to drive
    E. he obtains the names and addresses of drivers and witnesses

21. A detective, following a tip that a notorious bank robber is to meet a woman in a certain restaurant, is seated in a booth from which he can observe people entering and leaving. While waiting, he notices a flashily dressed woman get up from a table and slip by the cashier without paying her check. The detective ignored the incident and continued watching for the wanted man.
    This course of action was
    A. *correct*; the woman probably forgot to pay her bill
    B. *incorrect*; he should have arrested the woman since a *bird in the hand is worth two in the bush*
    C. *correct*; it is not the duty of the police department to protect businessmen from loss due to their own negligence
    D. *incorrect*; he should have followed the woman since she may lead to the bank robber
    E. *correct*; the detective should not risk losing the bank robber by checking on this incident

6 (#1)

22. All officers are required to maintain a record of their daily police activity in a memorandum book.
　　The LEAST likely reason for this requirement is to
　　　A. make it unnecessary for the officer to remember police incidents
　　　B. give supervisors information concerning the officer's daily work
　　　C. serve as a possible basis to refute unjustified complaints against the officer
　　　D. make a record of information that may have a bearing on a court action
　　　E. record any action which may later require an explanation

22.____

23. Police officers have a duty to take into custody any person who is actually or apparently mentally ill.
　　Of the following cases, the one LEAST likely to fall under this provision of the law is the
　　　A. quarrelsome person who makes unjustifiable accusations
　　　B. elderly man who appears confused and unable to dress or feed himself
　　　C. young man who sits on the sidewalk curb staring into space and, when questioned, gives meaningless answers
　　　D. man who shouts obscenities at strangers in the streets
　　　E. woman who accuses waiters of attempting to poison her

23.____

24. An officer should not take notes while first questioning a suspect.
　　Of the following, the MOST important reason for this procedure is that
　　　A. information obtained at this time will probably not be truthful
　　　B. unessential facts can be eliminated if statements are written late
　　　C. the physical reactions of the suspect during interrogation can be better observed
　　　D. the exact wording is of no importance
　　　E. the statement will be better organized if written later

24.____

25. An officer should know the occupations and habits of the people on his beat. In heavily populated districts, however, it is too much to ask that the officer know all the people on his beat.
　　If this statement is correct, the one of the following which would be the MOST practical course for an officer to follow is to
　　　A. concentrate on becoming acquainted with the oldest residents of the beat
　　　B. limit his attention to people who work as well as live in the district
　　　C. limit his attention to people with criminal records
　　　D. concentrate on becoming acquainted with key people such as janitors, bartenders, and local merchants
　　　E. concentrate on becoming acquainted with the newest residents of the beat

25.____

26. An officer off-duty but in uniform recognizes a stolen car parked outside of a tavern. He notices that the radiator of the car is warm, indicating recent use.
　　Of the following, the MOST practical course for the officer to follow is to
　　　A. enter the tavern and ask aloud for the driver of the car
　　　B. stand in a nearby doorway and watch the car

26.____

C. search for the officer on the beat and report the facts to him
D. telephone the station house as soon as he arrives home
E. enter the tavern and privately ask the bartender if he knows who owns the car

27. When a person is arrested, he is always asked whether he uses narcotics, regardless of the charge against him.
    Of the following, the MOST important reason for asking this question is that
    A. drug addicts can be induced to confess by withholding narcotics from them
    B. the theft of narcotics is becoming a serious police problem
    C. criminals are usually drug addicts
    D. many drug addicts commit crimes in order to obtain money for the purchase of narcotics
    E. it may be possible to convict the suspect of violation of the narcotics law

28. Of the following types of crimes, increased police vigilance would probably be LEAST successful in preventing
    A. murder   B. burglary   C. prostitution
    D. automobile thefts   E. robbery

29. The Police Department has been hiring civilian women to direct traffic at school crossings.
    The MOST important reason for this policy is
    A. to stimulate civic interest in police problems
    B. to dramatize the traffic safety problem
    C. that women are more careful of the safety of children
    D. that young school children have more confidence in women who are mothers of their playmates
    E. to free policemen for regular patrol duty

30. Of the following, the fact that makes it MOST difficult to identify stolen cars is that
    A. thieves frequently damage stolen cars
    B. many cars are similar in appearance
    C. thieves frequently disguise stolen cars
    D. owners frequently don't report stolen cars which are covered by insurance
    E. owners frequently delay reporting the theft

31. When testifying in a criminal case, it is MOST important that a policeman endeavor to
    A. avoid technical terms which may be unfamiliar to the jury
    B. lean over backwards in order to be fair to the defendant
    C. assist the prosecutor even if some exaggeration is necessary
    D. avoid contradicting other prosecution witnesses
    E. confine his answers to the questions asked

32. When investigating a burglary, a policeman should obtain as complete descriptions as possible of articles of value which were stolen, but should list, without describing, stolen articles which are relatively valueless.
This suggested procedure is
    A. *poor*; what is valueless to one person may be of great value to another
    B. *good*; it enables the police to concentrate on recovering the most valuable articles
    C. *poor*; articles of little value frequently provide the only evidence connecting the suspect to the crime
    D. *good*; the listing of the inexpensive items is probably incomplete
    E. *poor*; the police should make the same effort to recover all stolen property, regardless of value

33. At 10 A.M. on a regular school day, an officer notices a boy about 11 years old wandering in the street. When asked the reason he is not in school, he replies that he attends school in the neighborhood, but that he felt sick that morning. The officer then took the boy to the principal of the school.
This method of handling the situation was
    A. *bad*; the officer should have obtained verification of the boy's illness
    B. *good*; the school authorities are best equipped to deal with the problem
    C. *bad*; the officer should have obtained the boy's name and address and reported the incident to the attendance officer
    D. *good*; seeing the truant boy escorted by an officer will deter other children from truancy
    E. *bad*; the principal of a school should not be saddled with a truancy problem

34. During an investigation of a robbery, an officer caught one of the witnesses contradicting himself on one point. Upon questioning, the witness readily admitted the contradiction.
The officer should conclude that
    A. the witness was truthful but emotionally disturbed by the experience
    B. all of the statements of the witness should be disregarded as untrustworthy
    C. the statements of the witness should be investigated carefully
    D. the witness was trying to protect the guilty person
    E. contradictions of this sort are inevitable

35. A woman was found dead by her estranged husband in the kitchen of a ground floor apartment. The husband stated that, although the apartment was full of gas and tightly closed, all the burners of the kitchen range were shut. The husband had gone to the apartment to get some clothes. When an officer arrived, the apartment was still heavy with gas fumes.
Of the following, the MOST likely explanation for these circumstances is that
    A. gas seeped into the apartment under the door from a defective gas furnace in the basement
    B. the husband has given false information to mislead the police

C. the woman changed her mind about committing suicide and shut off the jets just before she collapsed
D. a leak in the kitchen range had developed
E. the woman had died from some other cause than asphyxiation

36. An officer on post hears a cry for help from a woman in a car with two men. He approaches the car and is told by the woman that the men are kidnapping her. The men claim to be the woman's husband and doctor and state that they are taking her to a private mental hospital.
Of the following, the BEST course for the officer is to
    A. take all of them to the station house for further questioning
    B. permit the woman to depart and arrest the men
    C. call for an ambulance to take the woman to the nearest city mental hospital
    D. accompany the car to the private mental hospital
    E. permit the car to depart on the basis of the explanation

36._____

37. Social security cards are not acceptable proof of identification for police purposes.
Of the following, the MOST important reason for this rule is that the social security card
    A. is easily obtained
    B. states on its face *for social security purposes—not for identification*
    C. is frequently lost
    D. does not contain the address of the person
    E. does not contain a photograph, description, or fingerprints of the person

37._____

38. Many well-meaning people have proposed that officers in uniform not be permitted to arrest juveniles.
This proposal is
    A. *good*; the police are not equipped to handle juvenile offenders
    B. *bad*; juvenile offenders would lose respect for all law enforcement agencies
    C. *good*; offending juveniles should be segregated from hardened criminals
    D. *bad*; frequently it is the uniformed officer who first comes upon the youthful offender
    E. *good*; contact with the police would prevent any rehabilitative measures from being taken

38._____

39. An off-duty police officer was seated in a restaurant when two men entered, drew guns, and robbed the cashier. The officer made no effort to prevent the robbery or apprehend the criminals. Later he justified his conduct by stating that an officer when off-duty is a private citizen with the same duties and rights of all private citizens.
The officer's conduct was
    A. *wrong*; an officer must act to prevent crimes and apprehend criminals at all times
    B. *right*; he was out of uniform at the time of the robbery
    C. *wrong*; he had his gun with him at the time of the robbery

39._____

D. *right*; it would have been foolhardy for him to intervene when outnumbered by armed robbers
E. *wrong*; he should have obtained the necessary information and descriptions after the robbers left

40. Drivers with many convictions for traffic law violations sometimes try to conceal this record by cutting off the lower part of the operator's license and attaching to it clean section from a blank application form.
An officer who stops a driver and notices that his operator's license is torn and held together by transparent tape should FIRST
    A. verify the driver's explanation of the torn license
    B. examine both parts of the license to see if they match
    C. request additional proof of identity
    D. check the records of the Bureau of Motor Vehicles for unanswered summonses

Question 41-60.

DIRECTIONS: In answering Questions 41 through 60 select the lettered word or phrase which means MOST NEARLY the same as the word in capitals.

41. IMPLY
    A. agree to   B. hint at   C. laugh at
    D. mimic   E. reduce

42. APPRAISAL
    A. allowance   B. composition C. prohibition
    D. quantity   E. valuation

43. DISBURSE
    A. approve   B. expend   C. prevent
    D. relay   E. restrict

44. POSTERITY
    A. back payment   B. current procedure   C. final effort
    D. future generations E. rare specimen

45. PUNCTUAL
    A. clear   B. honest   C. polite
    D. prompt   E. prudent

46. PRECARIOUS
    A. abundant   B. alarmed   C. cautious
    D. insecure   E. placid

47. FOSTER
    A. delegate   B. demote   C. encourage
    D. plead   E. surround

48. PINNACLE
    A. center   B. crisis   C. outcome
    D. peak   E. personificaton
    48.____

49. COMPONENT
    A. flattery   B. opposite   C. part
    D. revision   E. trend
    49.____

50. SOLICIT
    A. ask   B. prohibit   C. promise
    D. revoke   E. surprise
    50.____

51. LIAISON
    A. asset   B. coordination   C. difference
    D. policy   E. procedure
    51.____

52. ALLEGE
    A. assert   B. break   C. irritate
    D. reduce   E. wait
    52.____

53. INFILTRATION
    A. consumption   B. disposal   C. enforcement
    D. penetration   E. seizure
    53.____

54. SALVAGE
    A. announce   B. combine   C. prolong
    D. save   E. try
    54.____

55. MOTIVE
    A. attack   B. favor   C. incentive
    D. patience   E. tribute
    55.____

56. PROVOKE
    A. adjust   B. incite   C. leave
    D. obtain   E. practice
    56.____

57. SURGE
    A. branch   B. contract   C. revenge
    D. rush   E. want
    57.____

58. MAGNIFY
    A. attract   B. demand   C. generate
    D. increase   E. puzzle
    58.____

59. PREPONDERANCE
    A. decision   B. judgment   C. outweighing
    D. submission   E. warning
    59.____

60. ABATE
    A. assist
    B. coerce
    C. diminish
    D. indulge
    E. trade

Question 61-65.

DIRECTIONS: Questions 61 through 65 are to be answered on the basis of the table which appears below.

VALUE OF PROPERTY STOLEN – 2019 AND 2020
LARCENY

Category	2019		2020	
	Number of Offenses	Value of Stolen Property	Number of Offenses	Value of Stolen Property
Pocket-picking	20	$1,950	10	$950
Purse-snatching	175	5,750	20	12,500
Shoplifting	155	7,950	225	17,350
Automobile thefts	1,040	127,050	860	108,000
Thefts of auto accessories	1,135	34,950	970	24,400
Bicycle thefts	355	8,250	240	6,350
All other thefts	1,375	187,150	1,300	153,150

61. Of the total number of larcenies reported for 2019, automobile thefts accounted for MOST NEARLY
    A. 5%   B. 15%   C. 25%   D. 50%   E. 75%

62. The LARGEST percentage decrease in the value of the stolen property from 2019 to 2020 was in the category of
    A. pocket-picking
    B. automobile thefts
    C. thefts of auto accessories
    D. bicycle thefts
    E. all other thefts

63. In 2020, the average amount of each theft was LOWEST for the category of
    A. pocket-picking
    B. purse-snatching
    C. shoplifting
    D. thefts of auto accessories

64. The category which had the LARGEST numerical reduction in the number of offenses from 2019 to 2020 was
    A. pocket-picking
    B. automobile thefts
    C. thefts of auto accessories
    D. bicycle thefts
    E. all other thefts

65. When the categories are ranked for each year, according to the number of offenses committed in each category (largest number to rank first), the number of categories which will have the same rank in 2019 as in 2020 is
    A. 3   B. 4   C. 5   D. 6   E. 7

13 (#1)

66. A parade is marching up an avenue for 60 city blocks. A sample count of the number of people watching the parade on one side of the street in the block is taken, first, in a block near the end of the parade, and then in a block at the middle; the former count is 4,000 and the latter is 6,000.
If the average for the entire parade is assumed to be the average of the two samples, then the estimated number of persons watching the entire parade is MOST NEARLY
   A. 240,000   B. 300,000   C. 480,000   D. 600,000   E. 720,000

66.____

67. Suppose that the revenue from parking meters in a city was 5% greater in 2019 than in 2018, and 2% less in 2020 than in 2019.
If the revenue in 2018 was $1,500,000, then the revenue in 2020 was
   A. $1,541,500   B. $1,542,000   C. $1,542,500
   D. $1,543,000   E. $1,543,500

67.____

68. A radio motor patrol car completes a ten mile trip in twenty minutes.
If it does one-half the distance at a speed of twenty miles an hour, its speed, in miles per hour, for the remainder of the distance must be
   A. 30   B. 40   C. 50   D. 60   E. 70

68.____

69. A public beach has two parking areas. Their capacities are in the ratio of two to one and, on a certain day, are filled to 60% and 40% of capacity, respectfully.
The entire parking facilities of the beach on that day are MOST NEARLY _____ filled.
   A. 38%   B. 43%   C. 48%   D. 53%   E. 58%

69.____

70. While on foot patrol, an officer walks north for eleven blocks, turns around and walks south for six blocks, turns around and walks north for two blocks, then makes a right turn and walks one block.
In relation to his starting point, he is now _____ blocks away and facing _____.
   A. twenty; east   B. eight; east   C. seven; west
   D. nine; north   E. seven; north

70.____

Question 71-73.

DIRECTIONS: Questions 71 through 73 are to be answered on the basis of the following paragraph.

   When police officers search for a stolen car, they first check for the color of the car, then for make, model, year, body damage, and finally license number. The first five can be detected from almost any angle, while the recognition of the license number is often not immediately apparent. The serial number and motor number, though less likely to be changed than the easily substituted license number, cannot be observed in initial detection of the stolen car.

71. According to the above paragraph, the one of the following features which is LEAST readily observed in checking for a stolen car in moving traffic is
   A. license number   B. serial number   C. model
   D. make   E. color

71.____

72. The feature of a car that cannot be determined from most angles of observation is the
    A. make B. model C. year
    D. license number E. color

73. Of the following, the feature of a stolen car that is MOST likely to be altered by a car thief shortly after the car is stolen is the
    A. license number B. motor number C. color
    D. model E. minor body damage

Question 74-75.

DIRECTIONS: Questions 74 and 75 are to be answered on the basis of the following paragraph.

The racketeer is primarily concerned with business affairs, legitimate or otherwise, and preferably those which are close to the margin of legitimacy. He gets his best opportunities from business organizations which meet the need of large sections of the public for goods or services which are defined as illegitimate by the same public, such as prostitution, gambling, illicit drugs or liquor. In contrast to the thief, the racketeer and the establishments he controls deliver goods and services for money received.

74. From the above paragraph, it can be deduced that suppression of racketeers is difficult because
    A. victims of racketeers are not guilty of violating the law
    B. racketeers are generally engaged in fully legitimate enterprises
    C. many people want services which are not obtainable through legitimate sources
    D. the racketeers are well organized
    E. laws prohibiting gambling and prostitution are unenforceable

75. According to the above paragraph, racketeering, unlike theft, involves
    A. objects of value B. payment for goods received
    C. organized gangs D. public approval
    E. unlawful activities

Question 76-78.

DIRECTIONS: Questions 76 through 78 are to be answered on the basis of the following paragraph.

A number of crimes, such as robbery, assault, rape, certain forms of theft and burglary, are highly visible crimes in that it is apparent to all concerned that they are criminal acts prior to or at the time they are committed. In contrast to these, check forgeries, especially those committed by first offenders, have low visibility. There is little in the criminal act or in the interaction between the check passer and the person cashing the check to identify it as a crime. Closely related to this special quality of the forgery crime is the fact that, while it is formally defined and treated as a felonious or infamous crime, it is informally held by the legally untrained public to be a relatively harmless form of crime.

76. According to the above paragraph, crimes of high visibility
    A. are immediately recognized as crimes by the victims
    B. take place in public view
    C. always involve violence or the threat of violence
    D. usually are committed after dark
    E. can be observed from a distance

77. According to the above paragraph,
    A. the public regards check forgery as a minor crime
    B. the law regards check forgery as a minor crime
    C. the law distinguishes between check forgery and other forgery
    D. it is easier to spot inexperienced check forgers than other criminals
    E. it is more difficult to identify check forgers than other criminals

78. As used in the above paragraph, an *infamous* crime is
    A. a crime attracting great attention from the public
    B. more serious than a felony
    C. less serious than a felony
    D. more or less serious than a felony, depending upon the surrounding circumstances
    E. the same as a felony

Question 79-81.

DIRECTIONS: Questions 79 through 81 are to be answered on the basis of the following paragraph.

Criminal science is largely the science of identification. Progress in this field has been marked and sometimes very spectacular because new techniques, instruments, and facts flow continuously from the scientist. But the crime laboratories are undermanned, trade secrets still prevail, and inaccurate conclusions are often the result. However, modern gadgets cannot substitute for the skilled intelligent investigator; he must be their master.

79. According to the above paragraph, criminal science
    A. excludes the field of investigation
    B. is primarily interested in establishing identity
    C. is based on the equipment used in crime laboratories
    D. uses techniques different from those used in other sciences
    E. is essentially secret in nature

80. Advances in criminal science have been, according to the above paragraph,
    A. extremely limited   B. slow but steady
    C. unusually reliable   D. outstanding
    E. infrequently worthwhile

81. A problem that has not been overcome completely in crime work is, according to the above paragraph, 81._____
    A. unskilled investigators
    B. the expense of new equipment and techniques
    C. an insufficient number of personnel in crime laboratories
    D. inaccurate equipment used in laboratories
    E. conclusions of the public about the value of this field

Question 82-84.

DIRECTIONS: Questions 82 through 84 are to be answered on the basis of the following paragraph.

The New York City Police Department will accept for investigation no report of a person missing from his residence if such residence is located outside of New York City. The person reporting same will be advised to report such fact to the police department of the locality where the missing person lives, which will, if necessary, communicate officially with the New York City Police Department. However, a report will be accepted of a person who is missing from a temporary residence in New York City, but the person making the report will be instructed to make a report also to the police department of the locality where the missing person lives.

82. According to the above paragraph, a report to the New York City Police Department of a missing person whose permanent residence is outside of New York City will 82._____
    A. always be investigated provided that a report is also made to his local police authorities
    B. never be investigated unless requested officially by his local police authorities
    C. be investigated in cases of temporary New York City residence, but a report should always be made to his local police authorities
    D. be investigated if the person making the report is a New York City resident
    E. always be investigated and a report will be made to the local police authorities by the New York City Police Department

83. Of the following, the MOST likely reason for the procedure described in the above paragraph is that 83._____
    A. non-residents are not entitled to free police service from New York City
    B. local police authorities would resent interference in their jurisdiction
    C. local police authorities sometimes try to unload their problems on the New York City Police
    D. local police authorities may be better able to conduct an investigation
    E. few persons are erroneously reported as missing

84. Mr. Smith, who lives in Jersey City, and Mr. Jones, who lives in Newark, arrange to meet in New York City, but Mr. Jones does not keep the appointment. Mr. Smith telephones Mr. Jones several times the next day and gets no answer. Mr. Smith believes that something has happened to Mr. Jones. 84._____

According to the above paragraph, Mr. Smith should apply to the police authorities of
A. Jersey City
B. Newark
C. Newark and New York City
D. Jersey City and New York City
E. Newark, Jersey City, and New York City

Question 85-87.

DIRECTIONS: Questions 85 through 87 are to be answered on the basis of the following paragraph.

Some early psychologists believed that the basic characteristic of the criminal type was inferiority of intelligence, if not outright feeblemindedness. They were misled by the fact that they had measurements for all kinds of criminals but, until World War I gave them a draft army sample, they had no information on a comparable group of non-criminal adults. As soon as acceptable measurements could be taken of criminals and a comparable group of non-criminals, concern with feeblemindedness or with low intelligence as a type took on less and less significance in research in criminology.

85. According to the above paragraph, some early psychologists were in error because they did not
    A. distinguish among the various types of criminals
    B. devise a suitable method of measuring intelligence
    C. measure the intelligence of non-criminals as a basis for comparison
    D. distinguish between feeblemindedness and inferiority of intelligence
    E. clearly define the term *intelligence*

86. The above paragraph implies that studies of the intelligence of criminals and non-criminals
    A. are useless because it is impossible to obtain comparable groups
    B. are not meaningful because only the less intelligent criminals are detected
    C. indicate that criminals are more intelligent than non-criminals
    D. indicate that criminals are less intelligent than non-criminals
    E. do not indicate that there are any differences between the two groups

87. According to the above paragraph, studies of World War I draft gave psychologists vital information concerning
    A. adaptability to army life of criminals and non-criminals
    B. criminal tendencies among draftees
    C. the intelligence scores of large numbers of men
    D. differences between intelligence scores of draftees and volunteers
    E. the behavior of men under abnormal conditions

Question 88-90.

DIRECTIONS: Questions 88 through 90 are to be answered on the basis of the following paragraph.

The use of a roadblock is simply an adaptation to police practices of the military concept of encirclement. Successful operation of a roadblock plan depends almost entirely on the amount of advance study and planning given to such operations. A thorough and detailed examination of the roads and terrain under the jurisdiction of a given police agency should be made with the locations of the roadblocks pinpointed in advance The first principle to be borne in mind in the location of each roadblock is the time element. Its location must be at a point beyond which the fugitive could not have possibly traveled in the time elapsed from the commission of the crime to the arrival of the officers at the roadblock.

88. According to the above paragraph,
    A. military operations have made extensive use of roadblocks
    B. the military concept of encirclement is an adaptation of police use of roadblocks
    C. the technique of encirclement has been widely used by military forces
    D. a roadblock is generally more effective than encirclement
    E. police use of roadblocks is based on the idea of military encirclement

89. According to the above paragraph,
    A. the factor of time is the sole consideration in the location of a roadblock
    B. the maximum speed possible in the method of escape is of major importance in roadblock location
    C. the time of arrival of officers at the site of a proposed roadblock is of little importance
    D. if the method of escape is not known, it should be assumed that the escape is by automobile
    E. a roadblock should be sited as close to the scene of the crime as the terrain will permit

90. According to the above paragraph,
    A. advance study and planning are of minor importance in the success of roadblock operations
    B. a thorough and detailed examination of all roads within a radius of fifty miles should precede the determination of a roadblock location
    C. consideration of terrain features is important in planning the location of roadblocks
    D. the pinpointing of roadblocks should be performed before any advance study is made
    E. a roadblock operation can seldom be successfully undertaken by a single police agency

KEY (CORRECT ANSWERS)

1. E	21. E	41. B	61. C	81. C
2. C	22. A	42. E	62. A	82. C
3. A	23. A	43. B	63. D	83. D
4. A	24. C	44. D	64. B	84. B
5. D	25. D	45. D	65. C	85. C
6. C	26. B	46. D	66. D	86. E
7. B	27. D	47. C	67. E	87. C
8. A	28. A	48. D	68. D	88. E
9. C	29. E	49. C	69. D	89. B
10. A	30. C	50. A	70. B	90. C
11. D	31. E	51. B	71. B	
12. A	32. C	52. A	72. D	
13. E	33. B	53. D	73. A	
14. E	34. C	54. D	74. C	
15. E	35. B	55. C	75. B	
16. A	36. A	56. B	76. A	
17. B	37. E	57. D	77. A	
18. E	38. D	58. D	78. E	
19. B	39. A	59. C	79. B	
20. C	40. B	60. C	80. D	

EXAMINATION SECTION

TEST 1

DIRECTIONS: Each question or incomplete statement is followed by several suggested answers or completions. Select the one that BEST answers the question or completes the statement. *PRINT THE LETTER OF THE CORRECT ANSWER IN THE SPACE AT THE RIGHT.*

1. Upon arriving at the scene of an accident in which a pedestrian was struck and killed by an automobile, an officer's first action was to clear the scene of spectators.
   Of the following, the PRINCIPAL reason for this action is that
   A. important evidence may be inadvertently destroyed by the crowd
   B. this is a fundamental procedure in first aid work
   C. the operator of the vehicle may escape in the crowd
   D. witnesses will speak more freely if other persons are not present

   1.____

2. In questioning witnesses, an officer is instructed to avoid leading questions or questions that will suggest the answer.
   Accordingly, when questioning a witness about the appearance of a suspect, it would be BEST for him to ask:
   A. What kind of hat did he wear?   B. Did he wear a felt hat?
   C. What did he wear?   D. Didn't he wear a hat?

   2.____

3. The only personal description the police have of a particular criminal was made several years ago.
   Of the following, the item in the description that will be MOST useful in identifying him at the present time is the
   A. color of his eyes   B. color of his hair
   C. number of teeth   D. weight

   3.____

4. Crime statistics indicate that property crimes such as larceny, burglary, and robbery are more numerous during winter months than in summer.
   The one of the following explanations that MOST adequately accounts for this situation is that
   A. human needs, such as clothing, food, heat, and shelter, are greater in winter
   B. criminal tendencies are aggravated by climatic changes
   C. there are more hours of darkness in winter and such crimes are usually committed under cover of darkness
   D. urban areas are more densely populated during winter months, affording greater opportunity for such crimes

   4.____

5. When automobile tire tracks are to be used as evidence, a plaster cast is made of them.
   Of the following, the MOST probable reason for taking a photograph is that
   A. photographs can be duplicated more easily than castings
   B. less skill is required for photographing than casting
   C. the tracks may be damaged in the casting process
   D. photographs are more easily transported than castings

6. It is generally recommended that an officer, in lifting a revolver that is to be sent to the police laboratory for ballistics tests and fingerprint examination, do so by insetting a pencil through the trigger guard rather than into the barrel of the weapon.
   The reason for preferring this procedure is that
   A. every precaution must be taken not to eliminate fingerprints on the weapon
   B. there is a danger of accidentally discharging the weapon by placing the pencil in the barrel
   C. the pencil may make scratches inside the barrel that will interfere with the ballistics tests
   D. a weapon can more easily be lifted by the trigger guard

7. PHYSICIAN is to PATIENT as ATTORNEY is to
   A. court   B. client   C. counsel   D. judge

8. JUDGE is to SENTENCE as JURY is to
   A. court   B. foreman   C. defendant   D. verdict

9. REVERSAL is to AFFIRMANCE as CONVICTION is to
   A. appeal   B. acquittal   C. error   D. mistrial

10. GENUINE is to TRUE as SPURIOUS is to
    A. correct   B. conceived   C. false   D. speculative

11. ALLEGIANCE is to LOYALTY as TREASON is to
    A. felony   B. faithful   C. obedience   D. rebellion

12. CONCUR is to AGREE as DIFFER is to
    A. coincide   B. dispute   C. join   D. repeal

13. A person who has an uncontrollable desire to steal without need is called a
    A. dipsomaniac   B. kleptomaniac
    C. monomaniac   D. pyromaniac

14. In the sentence, "The placing of any inflammable substance in any building or the placing of any device or contrivence capable of producing fire, for the purpose of causing a fire is an attempt to burn," the MISSPELLED word is
    A. inflammable   B. substance   C. device   D. contrivence

3 (#1)

15. In the sentence, "The word 'break' also means obtaining an entrance into a building by any artifice used for that purpose, or by colussion with any person therein," the MISSPELLED word is
    A. obtaining   B. entrance   C. artifice   D. colussion

15.____

16. In the sentence, "Any person who with intent to provoke a breech of the peace causes a disturbance or is offensive to others may be deemed to have committed disorderly conduct," the MISSPELLED word is
    A. breech   B. disturbance   C. offensive   D. committed

16.____

17. In the sentence, "When the offender inflicts a grevious harm upon the person from whose possession, or in his presence, property is taken, he is guilty of robbery, the MISSPELLED word is
    A. offender   B. grevious   C. possession   D. presence

17.____

18. In the sentence, "A person who wilfully encourages or advises another person in attempting to take the latter's life is guilty of a felony," the MISSPELLED word is
    A. wilfully   B. encourages   C. advises   D. attempting

18.____

19. The treatment to be given the offender cannot alter the fact of his offense; but we can take measures to reduce the chances of similar acts in the future. We should banish the criminal, not in order to exact revenge nor directly to encourage reform, but to deter him and others from further illegal attacks on society.
    According to this paragraph, the PRINCIPAL reason for punishing criminals is to
    A. prevent the commission of future crimes
    B. remove them safely from society
    C. avenge society
    D. teach them that crime does not pay

19.____

20. Even the most comprehensive and best substantiated summaries of the total volume of criminal acts would not contribute greatly to an understanding of the varied social and biological factors which are sometimes assumed to enter into crime causation, nor would they indicate with any degree of precision the needs of police forces in combating crime.
    According to this statement,
    A. crime statistics alone do not determine the needs of police forces in combating crime
    B. crime statistics are essential to a proper understanding of the social factors of crime
    C. social and biological factor which enter the crime causation have little bearing on police needs
    D. a knowledge of the social and biological factors of crime is essential to a proper understanding of crime statistics

20.____

21. The police officer's art consists in applying and enforcing a multitude of laws and ordinances in such degree or proportion and in such manner that the greatest degree of social protection will be secured. The degree of enforcement and the method of application will vary with each neighborhood and community.
According to the foregoing paragraph,
   A. each neighborhood or community must judge for itself to what extent the law is to be enforced
   B. a police officer should only enforce those laws which are designed to give the greatest degree of social protection
   C. the manner and intensity of law enforcement is not necessarily the same in all communities
   D. all laws and ordinances must be enforced in a community with the same degree of intensity

22. Police control in the sense of regulating the details of police operations involves such matters as the technical means for so organizing the available personnel that competent police leadership, when secured, can operate effectively. It is concerned not so much with the extent to which popular controls can be trusted to guide and direct the course of police protection a with the administrative relationships which should exist between the component parts of the police organism.
According to the foregoing statement, police control is
   A. solely a matter of proper personnel assignment
   B. the means employed to guide and direct the course of police protection
   C. principally concerned with the administrative relationships between units of a police organization
   D. the sum total of means employed in rendering police protection

23. Two patrol cars hurry to the scene of an accident from different directions. The first proceeds at the rate of 45 miles per hour and arrives in four minutes. Although the second car travels over a route which is three-fourths of a mile longer, it arrives at the scene only a half-minute later.
The speed of the second car, expressed in miles per hour, is
   A. 50   B. 55   C. 60   D. 65

24. A motorcycle officer issued 72 traffic summonses in January, 60 in February and 83 in March.
In order to average 75 summonses per month for the four months of January, February, March, and April, during April he will have to issue _____ summonses.
   A. 80   B. 85   C. 90   D. 95

25. In a unit of the Police Department to which 40 officers are assigned, the sick report record during 2022 was as follows: 1 was absent 8 days, 5 were absent 3 days each, 4 were absent 5 days each, 10 were absent 2 days each, 8 were absent 4 days each, 5 were absent 1 day each.
The average number of days on sick report for all the members of this unit is MOST NEARLY
   A. ½   B. 1   C. 2 ½   D. 3

Questions 26-30.

DIRECTIONS: Column I lists various statements of fact. Column II is a list of crimes. Next to the numbers corresponding to the number preceding the statements of fact in Column I, place the letter preceding the crime listed in Column II with which Jones should be charged. In answering these questions, the following definitions of crimes should be applied, bearing in mind that ALL elements contained in the definitions must be present in order to charge a person with that crime.

BURGLARY is breaking and entering a building with intent to commit some crime therein. EMBEZZLEMENT is the appropriation to one's use of another's property which has been entrusted to one's care or which has come lawfully into one's possession. EXTORTION is taking or obtaining property from another with his consent, induced by a wrongful use of force or fear. LARCENY is taking and carrying away the personal property of another with intent to deprive or defraud the true owner of the use and benefit of such property. ROBBERY is the unlawful taking of the personal property of another from his person or in his presence by force or violence, or fear of injury.

COLUMN I

26. Jones, believing Smith had induced his wife to leave him, went to Smith's home armed with a knife with which he intended to assault Smith. When his knock was unanswered, he forced open the door of Smith's home and entered but, finding the house empty, he threw away the knife and left.

27. Jones was employed as a collection agent by Smith. When Smith refused to reimburse him for certain expenses he claimed to have incurred in connection with his work, Jones deducted this amount from sums he had collected for Smith.

28. Jones spent the night in a hotel. During the night he left his room, went downstairs to the desk, stole money and returned to his room.

29. Jones, a building inspector, found that the elevators in Smith's building were being operated without a permit. He threatened to report the matter and have the elevators shut down unless Smith paid him a sum of money. Smith paid the amount demanded

30. Jones held-up Smith on the street and, pointing a revolve at him, demanded his money. Smith, without resisting, handed Jones his money. When Jones was apprehended, it was discovered that the revolver was a toy.

COLUMN II

A. burglary
B. embezzlement
C. extortion
D. larceny
E. robbery
F. no crime

26.____
27.____
28.____
29.____
30.____

Questions 31-40.

DIRECTIONS: Questions 31 through 40 consist of statements from which a term is missing. Each of these statements can be completed correctly with one of the terms in the following list. In the space opposite the number corresponding to the number of the question, place the LETTER preceding the term in the following list which MOST accurately completes the statement.

A. affidavit
B. appeal
C. arraignment
D. arrest
E. bench warrant
F. habeas corpus
G. indictment
H. injunction
I. sentence
J. subpoena

31. A _____ is a writ calling witnesses to court. 31._____

32. _____ is a method used to obtain a review of a case in court of superior jurisdiction. 32._____

33. A judgment passed by a court on a person on trial as a criminal offender is called a _____. 33._____

34. _____ is a writ or order requiring a person to refrain from a particular act. 34._____

35. _____ is the name given to a writ commanding the bringing of the body of a certain person before a certain court. 35._____

36. A _____ is a court order directing that an offender be brought into court. 36._____

37. The calling of a defendant before the court to answer an accusation is called _____. 37._____

38. The accusation in writing, presented by the grand jury to a competent court charging a person with a public offense is an _____. 38._____

39. A sworn declaration in writing is an _____. 39._____

40. _____ is the taking of a person into custody for the purpose of holding him to answer a criminal charge. 40._____

Questions 41-55.

DIRECTIONS: Questions 41 through 55 consist of statements from which a term is missing. Each of these statements can be completed correctly with one of the terms in the following list. In the space opposite the number corresponding to the number of the question, place the LETTER preceding the term in the following list which MOST accurately completes the statement.

A. accessory B. accomplice C. alibi
D. autopsy E. ballistics F. capital
G. confidence man H. commission I. conspiracy
J. corroborated K. grand jury L. homicide
M. misdemeanors N. penology O. perjury

41. _____ is the dissection of a dead human body to determine the cause of death. 41._____

42. The general term which mean the killing of one person by another is _____. 42._____

43. _____ is the science of the punishment of crime. 43._____

44. False swearing constitutes the crime of _____. 44._____

45. A combination of two or more persons to accomplish a criminal or unlawful act is called _____. 45._____

46. By _____ is meant evidence showing that a defendant was in another place when the crime was committed. 46._____

47. _____ is a term frequently used to describe a person engaged in a kind of swindling operation. 47._____

48. A _____ offense is one for which a life sentence or death penalty is prescribed by law. 48._____

49. A violation of a law may be either an act of omission or an act of _____. 49._____

50. An _____ is a person who is liable to prosecution for the identical offense charged against a defendant on trial. 50._____

51. A person would be an _____ who after the commission of a crime aided in the escape of one he knew to be an offender. 51._____

52. An official body called to hear complaints and to determine whether there is ground for criminal prosecution is known as the _____. 52._____

53. Crimes are generally divided into two classes, namely felonies and _____. 53._____

54. _____ is the science of the motion of projectiles. 54._____

55. Testimony of a witness which is confirmed by another witness is _____. 55._____

Questions 56-60.

DIRECTIONS: Next to the question number which corresponds with the number of each item in Column I, place the letter preceding the adjective in Column II which BEST describes the persons in Column I.

COLUMN I	COLUMN II	
56. A talkative woman	A. abstemious	56.____
	B. pompous	
57. A person on a reducing diet	C. erudite	57.____
	D. benevolent	
58. A scholarly professor	E. docile	58.____
	F. loquacious	
59. A man who seldom speaks	G. indefatigable	59.____
	H. taciturn	
60. A charitable person		60.____

Questions 61-65.

DIRECTIONS: Next to the question number which corresponds with the number preceding each profession in Column I, place the letter preceding the word in Column II which BEST explains the subject of that profession.

COLUMN I	COLUMN II	
61. Geologist	A. animals	61.____
	B. eyes	
62. Oculist	C. feet	62.____
	D. fortune-telling	
63. Podiatrist	E. language	63.____
	F. rocks	
64. Palmist	G. stamps	64.____
	H. woman	
65. Zoologist		65.____

Questions 66-70.

DIRECTIONS: Next to the question number corresponding to the number of each of the words in Column I, place the letter preceding the word in Column II that is MOST NEARLY OPPOSITE to it in meaning.

COLUMN I	COLUMN II	
66. comely	A. beautiful	66.____
	B. cowardly	
67. eminent	C. kind	67.____
	D. sedate	
68. frugal	E. shrewd	68.____
	F. ugly	
69. gullible	G. unknown	69.____
	H. wasteful	
70. valiant		70.____

KEY (CORRECT ANSWERS)

1.	A	16.	A	31.	J	46.	C	61.	F
2.	C	17.	B	32.	B	47.	G	62.	B
3.	A	18.	A	33.	I	48.	F	63.	C
4.	C	19.	A	34.	H	49.	H	64.	D
5.	C	20.	A	35.	F	50.	B	65.	A
6.	C	21.	C	36.	E	51.	A	66.	F
7.	B	22.	C	37.	C	52.	L	67.	G
8.	D	23.	A	38.	G	53.	N	68.	H
9.	B	24.	B	39.	A	54.	E	69.	E
10.	C	25.	C	40.	D	55.	K	70.	B
11.	D	26.	A	41.	D	56.	F		
12.	B	27.	B	42.	M	57.	A		
13.	B	28.	D	43.	O	58.	C		
14.	D	29.	C	44.	P	59.	H		
15.	D	30.	E	45.	J	60.	D		

EVALUATING INFORMATION AND EVIDENCE
EXAMINATION SECTION
TEST 1

DIRECTIONS: Each question or incomplete statement is followed by several suggested answers or completions. Select the one that BEST answers the question or completes the statement. *PRINT THE LETTER OF THE CORRECT ANSWER IN THE SPACE AT THE RIGHT.*

Question 1-4.

DIRECTIONS: Questions 1 through 4 measure your ability (1) to determine whether statements from witnesses say essentially the same thing and (2) to determine the evidence needed to make it reasonably certain that a particular conclusion is true.
To do well in this part of the test, you do NOT have to have a working knowledge of police procedures and techniques or to have any more familiarity with crimes and criminal behavior than that acquired from reading newspapers, listening to radio, or watching TV. In order to do well in this part, you must read carefully and reason closely. Sloppy reading or sloppy reasoning will lead to a low score.

1. In which of the following do the two statements made say essentially the same thing in two different ways?
   I. All members of the pro-x group are free from persecution.
      No person that is persecuted is a member of the pro-x group.
   II. Some responsible employees of the police department are not supervisors.
       Some police department supervisors are not responsible employees.
   The CORRECT answer is:
   A. I only
   B. II only
   C. Both I and II
   D. Neither I nor II

1.____

2. In which the following do the two statements made say essentially the same thing in two different ways?
   I. All Nassau County police officers weigh less than 225 pounds.
      No police officer weighs more than 225 pounds.
   II. No police officer is an alcoholic.
       No alcoholic is a police officer.
   The CORRECT answer is:
   A. I only
   B. II only
   C. Both I and II
   D. Neither I nor II

2.____

3. <u>Summary of Evidence Collected to Date</u>: All pimps in the precinct own pink-colored cars and carry knives.
   <u>Prematurely Drawn Conclusion</u>: Any person in the precinct who carries a knife is a pimp.

3.____

93

Which one of the following additional pieces of evidence, if any, would make it *reasonably certain* that the conclusion drawn is TRUE?
- A. Each person who carries a knife owns a pink-colored car.
- B. All persons who own pink-colored cars pimp.
- C. No one who carries a knife has a vocation other than pimping.
- D. None of the above

4. Summary of Evidence Collected to Date:
   a. Some of the robbery suspects have served time as convicted felons.
   b. Some of the robbery suspects are female.
   Prematurely Drawn Conclusion: Some of the female suspects have never served time as convicted felons.
   Which one of the following additional pieces of evidence, if any, would make it *reasonably certain* that the conclusion drawn is TRUE?
   - A. The number of female suspects is the same as the number of robber suspects who have served time as convicted felons.
   - B. The number of female suspects is smaller than the number of convicted felons.
   - C. The number of suspects that have served time is smaller than the number of suspects that have been convicted of a felony.
   - D. None of the above

Questions 5-8.

DIRECTIONS: Questions 5 through 8 measure your ability to orient yourself within a given section of a town, neighborhood, or particular area. Each of the questions describes a starting point and a destination. Assume that you are driving a patrol car in the area shown on the map accompanying the questions. Use the map as a basis for choosing the shortest way to get from one point to another without breaking the law.

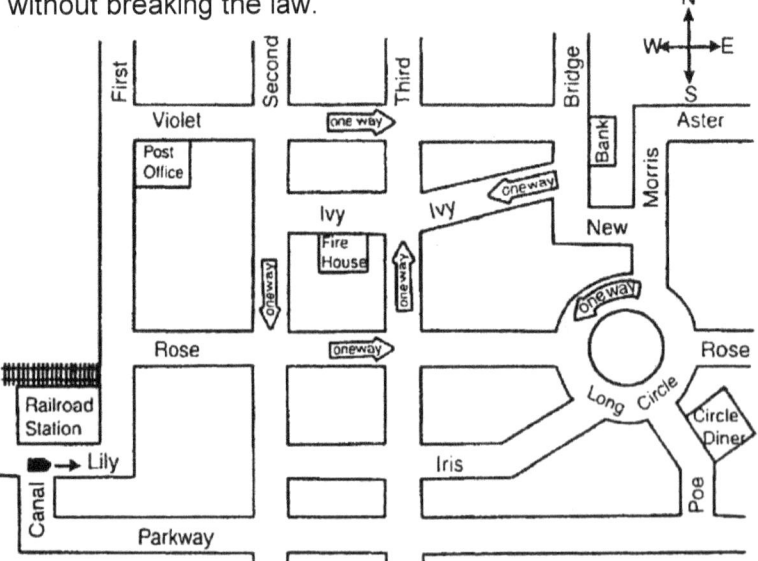

A street marked one way is one-way for the full length, even when there are breaks or jogs in the street. EXCEPTION: A street that does not have the same name over the full length.

5. A patrol car at the train station is sent to the bank to investigate a robbery. 5._____
   The SHORTEST way to get there without breaking any traffic laws is to go
   A. east on Lily, north on First, east on Rose, north on Third, and east on Ivy to bank
   B. east on Lily, north on First, east on Violet, and south on Bridge to bank
   C. south on Canal, east on Parkway, north on Poe, around Long Circle to Morris, west on New, and north on Bridge to bank
   D. south on Canal, east on Parkway, north on Third, and east on Ivy to bank

6. At the bank, the patrol car receives a call to hurry to the post office. 6._____
   The SHORTEST way to get there without breaking any traffic laws is to go
   A. west on Ivy, south on Second, west on Rose, and north on First to post office
   B. west on Ivy, south on Second, west on Rose, and south on First to post office
   C. south on Bridge, east on New, south on Morris, around Long Circle, south on Poe, west on Parkway, north on Canal, east on Lily, and north on First to post office
   D. north on Bridge, west on Violet, and south on First to post office

7. On leaving the post office, the police officers decide to go to the Circle Diner. 7._____
   The SHORTEST way to get there without breaking any traffic laws is to go
   A. south on First, left on Rose, right on Second, left on Parkway, and right on Poe to diner
   B. south on First, left on Rose, around Long Circle, and right on Poe to diner
   C. south on First, left on Rose, right on Second, right on Iris, around Long Circle, and left on Poe to diner
   D. west on Violet, right on Bridge, right on new, right on Morris, around Long Circle, and left on Poe to diner

8. During lunch break, a fire siren sounds and the police officers rush to their patrol 8._____
   car and head to the firehouse.
   The SHORTEST way to get there without breaking any traffic laws is to go
   A. north on Poe, around Long Circle, west on Iris, north on Third, and west on Ivy to firehouse
   B. north on Poe, around Long Circle,, north on Morris, west on New, north on Bridge, and west on Ivy to firehouse
   C. north on Poe, around Long Circle, west on Rose, north on Third, and west on Ivy to firehouse
   D. south on Poe, west on Parkway, north on Third, and east on Ivy to firehouse

Questions 9-13.

DIRECTIONS: Questions 9 through 13 measure your ability to understand written descriptions of events. Each question presents you with a description of an accident, a crime, or an event and asks you which of four drawings BEST represent it.

4 (#1)

In the drawings, the following symbols are used (these symbols and their meanings will be repeated in the test):

A moving vehicle is represented by this symbol: (front) ⬜ (rear)

A parked vehicle is represented by this symbol: (front) ◀■ (rear)

A pedestrian or a bicyclist is represented by this symbol: •

The path and direction of travel of a vehicle or pedestrian is indicated by a solid line: ⟶

EXCEPTION: The path and direction of travel of each vehicle or person directly involved in a collision from the point of impact is indicated by a dotted line: --→

9. A driver pulling out from between two parked cars on Magic is struck by a vehicle heading east which turns left onto Maple and flees. 9.____
Which of the following depicts the accident?

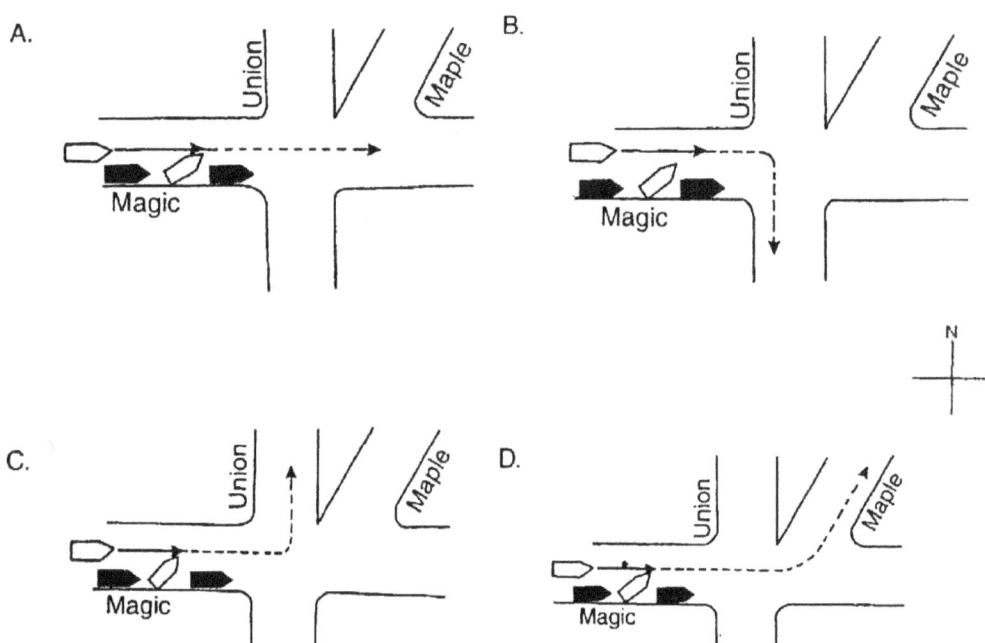

96

10. As Mr. Jones is driving south on Side St., he falls asleep at the wheel. His car goes out of control and sideswipes an oncoming car, goes through an intersection, and hits a pedestrian on the southeast corner of Main Street. Which of the following depicts the accident?

10.____

A.

B.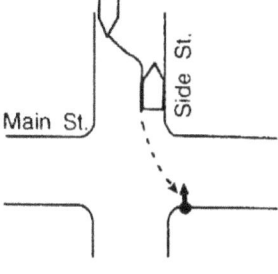

C.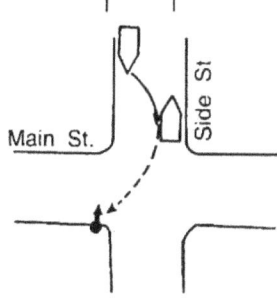

D.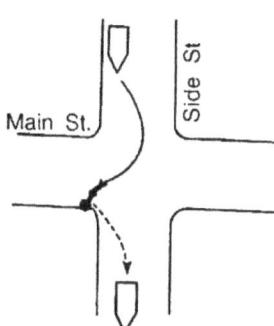

11. A car traveling south on Baltic skids through a red light at the intersection of Baltic and Atlantic, sideswipes a car stopped for a light in the northbound lane, skids 180 degrees, and stops on the west sidewalk of Baltic. Which of the following depicts the accident?

11.____

A.

B.

C.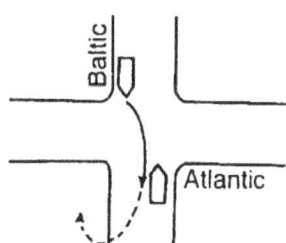

D.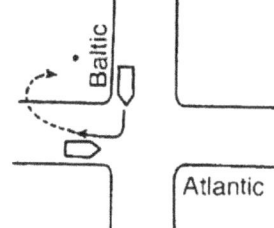

12. When found, the right front end of an automobile was smashed and bent around a post, and the hood was buckled.
Which of the following cars on a service lot is the car described?

A.
B.
C.
D.

13. An open floor safe with its door bet out of shape was found at the scene. It was empty. An electric drill and several envelopes and papers were found on the floor near the safe.
Which of the following shows the scene described?

A.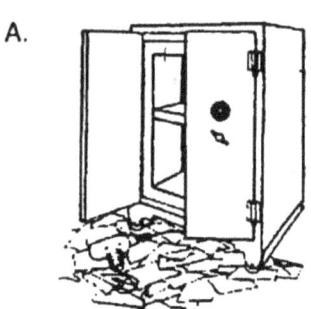
B.
C.
D.

Questions 14-16.

DIRECTIONS: In Questions 14 through 16, you are to pick the word or phrase CLOSEST in meaning to the word or phrase printed in capital letters.

14. HAZARDOUS
    A. uncertain   B. threatening   C. difficult   D. dangerous

15. NEGLIGENT
    A. careless   B. fearless   C. ruthless   D. useless

    15.____

16. PROVOKE
    A. accuse   B. arouse   C. insist   D. suspend

    16.____

Questions 17-20.

DIRECTIONS: Questions 17 through 20 measure your ability to do arithmetic related to police work. Each question presents a separate arithmetic problem to be solved.

17. To the nearest hour, how long can a specialized police vehicle with a 40-gallon fuel tank be on the road before heading for a service facility, assuming that the vehicle consumes 8 gallons per hour and must head for a service facility when there are only 8 gallons in the tank?
    A. 3   B. 4   C. 5   D. None of the above

    17.____

18. A man with a history of vagrancy was found dead under a bridge with the following U.S. currency in a band around his belly:
    7 $5 bills, 3 $10 bills, 11 $20 bills, 9 $50 bills, 4 $100 bills
    What is the TOTAL amount of the money that was found in the band?
    A. $1,015   B. $1,135   C. $2,719   D. None of the above

    18.____

19. X is 110 dimes; Y is 1,111 pennies.
    Which of the following statements about the values of X and Y above is TRUE?
    A. X is greater than Y.
    B. Y is greater than X.
    C. x equals Y.
    D. The relationship of X to Y cannot be determined from the information given.

    19.____

20. Which of the following individuals drinking hard liquor in a bar was 21 years old at the time of the incident?
    A. One born August 26, 1989. Date of incident is March 17, 2010.
    B. One born January 6, 1989. Date of incident is New Year's Eve 2009.
    C. One born 3/17/89. Date of incident is 2/14/10
    D. None of the above

    20.____

KEY (CORRECT ANSWERS)

1.	A	11.	C
2.	B	12.	D
3.	C	13.	B
4.	D	14.	D
5.	B	15.	A
6.	C	16.	B
7.	B	17.	B
8.	B	18.	B
9.	D	19.	B
10.	B	20.	D

EVALUATING INFORMATION AND EVIDENCE
EXAMINATION SECTION
TEST 1

DIRECTIONS: Each question or incomplete statement is followed by several suggested answers or completions. Select the one that BEST answers the question or completes the statement. *PRINT THE LETTER OF THE CORRECT ANSWER IN THE SPACE AT THE RIGHT.*

Questions 1-9.

DIRECTIONS: Questions 1 through 9 measure your ability to (1) determine whether statements from witnesses say essentially the same thing and (2) determine the evidence needed to make it reasonably certain that a particular conclusion is true.

1. Which of the following pairs of statements say essentially the same thing in two different ways?
    I. Some employees at the water department have fully vested pensions.
       At least one employee at the water department has a pension that is not fully vested.
    II. All swans are white birds.
        A bird that is not white is not a swan.
    The CORRECT answer is:
    A. I only   B. I and II   C. II only   D. Neither I nor II

    1.____

2. Which of the following pairs of statements say essentially the same thing in two different ways?
    I. If you live in Humboldt County, your property taxes are high.
       If your property taxes are high, you live in Humboldt County.
    II. All the Hutchinsons live in Lindsborg.
        At least some Hutchinsons do not live in Lindsborg.
    The CORRECT answer is;
    A. I only   B. I and II   C. II only   D. Neither I nor II

    2.____

3. Which of the following pairs of statements say essentially the same thing in two different ways?
    I. Although Spike is a friendly dog, he is also one of the most unpopular dogs on the block.
       Although Spike is one of the most unpopular dogs on the block, he is a friendly dog.
    II. Everyone in Precinct 19 is taller than Officer Banks.
        Nobody in Precinct 19 is shorter than Officer Banks.
    The CORRECT answer is:
    A. I only   B. I and II   C. II only   D. Neither I nor II

    3.____

4. Which of the following pairs of statements say essentially the same thing in two different ways?
   I. On Friday, every officer in Precinct 1 is assigned parking duty or crowd control, or both.
   If a Precinct 1 officer has been assigned neither parking duty nor crowd control, it is not Friday.
   II. Because the farmer mowed the hay fields today, his house will have mice tomorrow.
   Whenever the farmer mows his hay fields, his house has mice the next day.
   The CORRECT answer is:
   A. I only   B. I and II   C. II only   D. Neither I nor II

   4.____

5. Summary of Evidence Collected to Date:
   I. Fishing in the Little Pony River is against the law.
   Captain Rick caught an 8-inch trout and ate it for dinner.
   Prematurely Drawn Conclusion: Captain Rick broke the law.
   Which of the following pieces of evidence, if any, would make it reasonably certain that the conclusion drawn is true?
   A. Captain Rick caught his trout in the Little Pony River.
   B. There is no size limit on trout mentioned in the law.
   C. A trout is a species of fish.
   D. None of the above

   5.____

6. Summary of Evidence Collected to Date:
   I. Some of the doctors in the ICU have been sued for malpractice.
   II. Some of the doctors in the ICU are pediatricians.
   Prematurely Drawn Conclusion: Some of the pediatricians in the ICU have never been sued for malpractice.
   Which of the following pieces of evidence, if any, would make it reasonably certain that the conclusion drawn is true?
   A. The number of pediatricians in the ICU is the same as the number of doctors who have been sued for malpractice.
   B. The number of pediatricians in the ICU is smaller than the number of doctors who have been sued for malpractice.
   C. The number of ICU doctors who have been sued for malpractice is smaller than the number who are pediatricians.
   D. None of the above

   6.____

7. Summary of Evidence Collected to Date:
   I. Along Paseo Boulevard, there are five convenience stores.
   II. EZ-GO is east of Pop-a-Shop.
   III. Kwik-E-Mart is west of Bob's Market.
   IV. The Nightwatch is between EZ-GO and Kwik-E-Mart.
   Prematurely Drawn Conclusion: Pop-a-Shop is the westernmost convenience store on Paseo Boulevard.

   7.____

Which of the following pieces of evidence, if any, would make it reasonably certain that the conclusion drawn is true?
- A. Bob's Market is the easternmost convenience store on Paseo.
- B. Kwik-E-Mart is the second store from the west.
- C. The Nightwatch is west of the EZ-GO.
- D. None of the above

8. Summary of Evidence Collected to Date:
Stark drove home from work at 70 miles an hour and wasn't breaking the law.
Prematurely Drawn Conclusion: Stark was either on an interstate highway or in the state of Montana.
Which of the following pieces of evidence, if any, would make it reasonably certain that the conclusion drawn is true?
- A. There are no interstate highways in Montana.
- B. Montana is the only state that allows a speed of 70 miles an hour on roads other than interstate highways.
- C. Most states don't allow speed of 70 miles an hour on state highways.
- D. None of the above

9. Summary of Evidence Collected to Date:
   I. Margaret, owner of MetroWoman magazine, signed a contract with each of her salespeople promising an automatic $200 bonus to any employee who sells more than 60 subscriptions in a calendar month.
   II. Lynn sold 82 subscriptions to MetroWoman in the month of December.
Prematurely Drawn Conclusion: Lynn received a $20 bonus.
Which of the following pieces of evidence, if any, would make it reasonably certain that the conclusion is true?
- A. Lynn is a salesperson.
- B. Lynn works for Margaret.
- C. Margaret offered only $200 regardless of the number of subscriptions sold.
- D. None of the above

Questions 10-14.

DIRECTIONS: Questions 10 through 14 refer to Map #3 and measure your ability to orient yourself within a given section of town, neighborhood or particular area. Each of the questions describes a starting point and a destination. Assume that you are driving a car in the area shown on the map accompanying the questions. Use the map as a basis for the shortest way to get from one point to another without breaking the law.
On the map, a street marked by arrows, or by arrows and the words "One Way," indicates one-way travel and should be assumed to be one-way for the entire length, even when there are breaks or jogs in the street. EXCEPTION: A street that does not have the same name over the full length.

4 (#1)

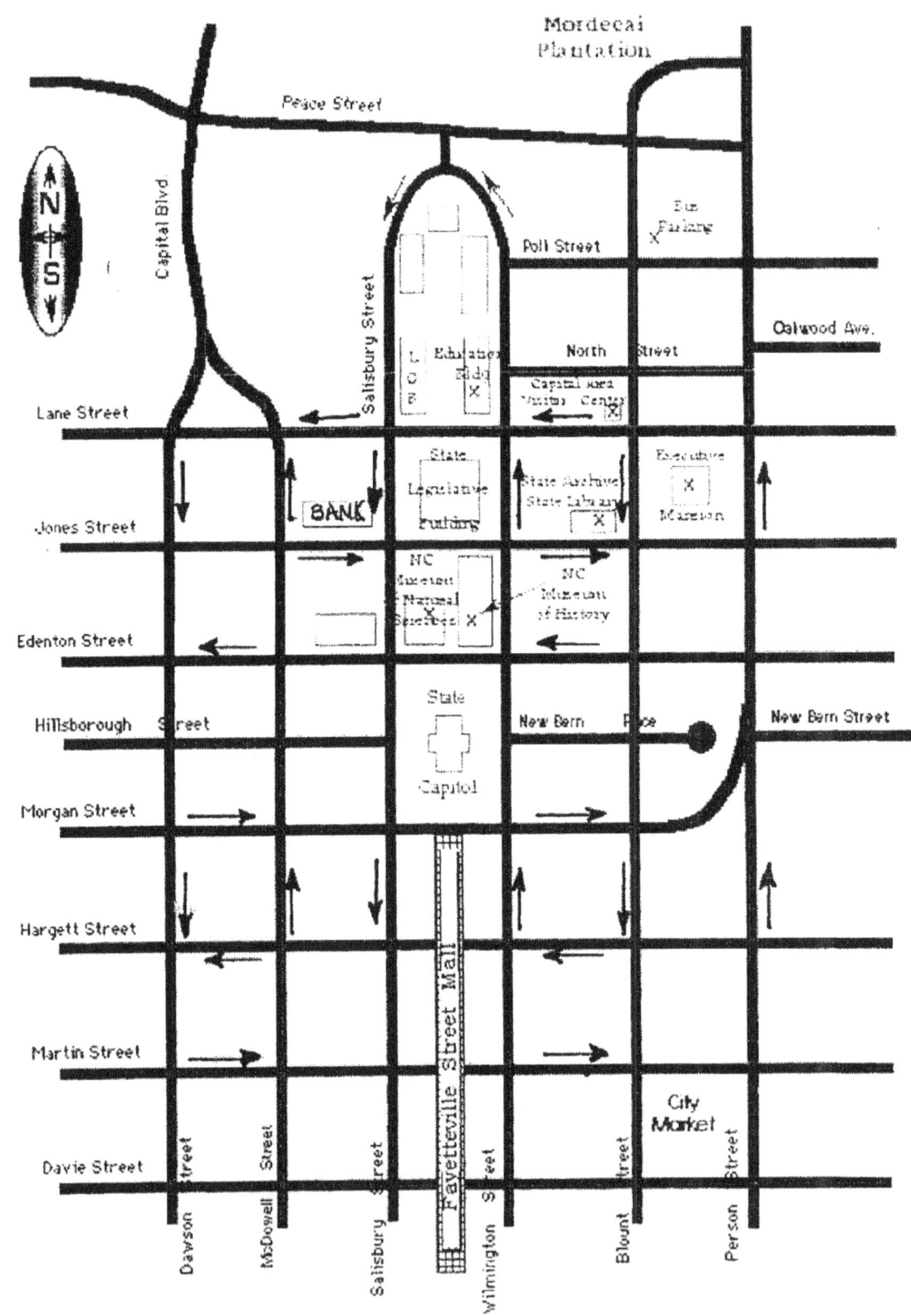

10. The SHORTEST legal way from the south end of the Fayetteville Street Mall, at Davie Street, to the city of Raleigh Municipal Building is
    A. west on Davie, north on McDowell
    B. west on Davie, north on Dawson
    C. east on Davie, north on Wilmington, west on Morgan
    D. east on Davie, north on Wilmington, west on Hargett

10._____

11. The SHORTEST legal way from the City Market to the Education Building is
    A. north on Blount, west on North
    B. north on Person, west on Lane
    C. north on Blount, west on Lane
    D. west on Martin, north on Wilmington

11._____

12. The SHORTEST legal way from the Education Building to the State Capitol is
    A. south on Wilmington
    B. north on Wilmington, west on Peace, south on Capitol, bear west to go south on Dawson, and east on Morgan
    C. west on Lane, south on Salisbury
    D. each on North, south on Blount, west on Edenton

12._____

13. The SHORTEST legal way from the State Capitol to Peace College is
    A. north on Wilmington, jog north, east on Peace
    B. east on Morgan, north on Person, west on Peace
    C. west on Edenton, north on McDowell, north on Capitol Blvd., east on Peace
    D. east on Morgan, north on Blount, west on Peace

13._____

14. The SHORTEST legal way from the State Legislative Building to the City Market is
    A. south on Wilmington, east on Martin
    B. east on Jones, south on Blount
    C. south on Salisbury, east on Davie
    D. east on Lane, south on Blount

14._____

Questions 15-19.

DIRECTIONS: Questions 15 through 19 refer to Figure #3, on the following page, and measure your ability to understand written descriptions of events. Each question presents a description of an accident or event and asks you which of the following five drawings in Figure #3 BEST represents it.
In the drawings, the following symbols are used:
Moving vehicle ⌂   Non-moving vehicle ▮
Pedestrian or bicyclist •
The path and direction of travel of a vehicle or pedestrian is indicated by a solid line.
The path and direction of travel of each vehicle or pedestrian directly involved in a collision from the point of impact is indicated by a dotted line.

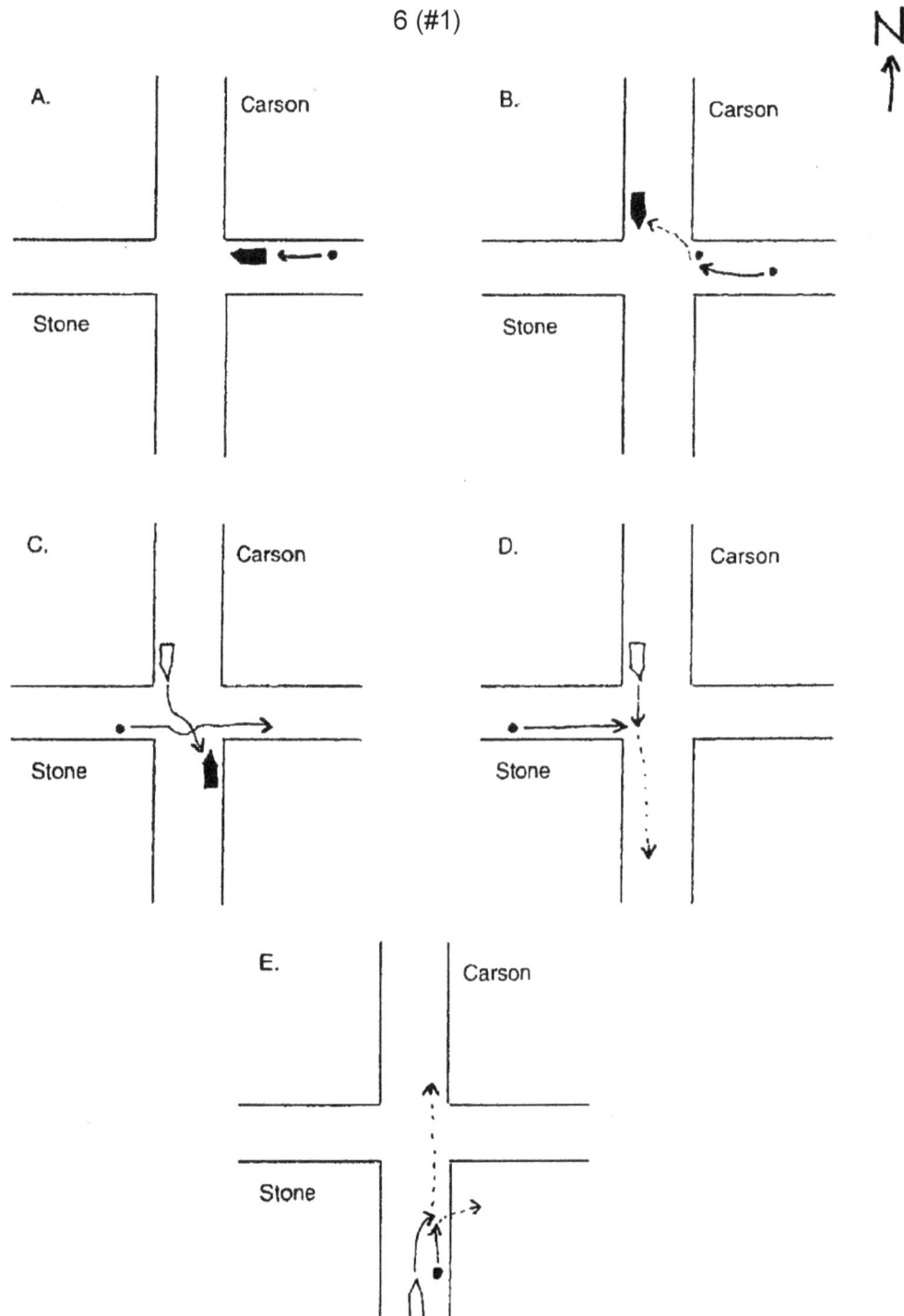

In the space at the right, print the letter of the drawing that BEST fit the descriptions written below.

15. A driver headed north on Carson veers to the right and strikes a bicyclist who is also headed north. The bicyclist is thrown from the road. The driver flees north on Carson.

15._____

16. A driver heading south on Carson runs the stop sign and barely misses colliding with an eastbound cyclist. The cyclist swerves to avoid the collision and continues traveling east. The driver swerves to avoid the collision and strikes a car parked in the northbound lane on Carson.

16.____

17. A bicyclist heading west on Stone collides with a pedestrian in the crosswalk, then veers through the intersection and collides with the front of a car parked in the southbound lane on Carson.

17.____

18. A driver traveling south on Carson runs over a bicyclist who has run the stop sign, and then flees south on Carson.

18.____

19. A bicyclist heading west on Stone collides with the rear of a car parked in the westbound lane.

19.____

Questions 20-22.

DIRECTIONS: In Questions 20 through 22, choose the word or phrase CLOSEST in meaning to the word or phrase printed in capital letters.

20. INSOLVENT
    A. bankrupt   B. vagrant   C. hazardous   D. illegal

20.____

21. TENANT
    A. laborer   B. occupant   C. owner   D. creditor

21.____

22. INFRACTION
    A. portion   B. violation   C. remark   D. detour

22.____

Questions 23-25.

DIRECTIONS: Questions 23 through 25 measure your ability to do fieldwork-related arithmetic. Each question presents a separate arithmetic problem for you to solve.

23. Officer Jones has served on the police force longer than Smith. Smith has served longer than Moore. Moore has served less time than Jones, and Park has served longer than Jones.
    Which officer has served the LONGEST on the police force?
    A. Jones   B. Smith   C. Moore   D. Park

23.____

24. A car wash has raised the price of an outside-only wash from $4 to $5. The car wash applies the same percentage increase to its inside-and-out wash, which was $10.
    What is the new cost of the inside-and-out wash?
    A. $8   B. $11   C. $12.50   D. $15

24.____

25. Ron and James, college students, make $10 an hour working at the restaurant. Ron works 13 hours a week and James works 20 hours a week.
To make the same amount that Ron earns in a year, James would work about _____ weeks.

   A. 18   B. 27   C. 34   D. 45

25._____

KEY (CORRECT ANSWERS)

1. C
2. D
3. B
4. B
5. A

6. D
7. B
8. B
9. B
10. A

11. B
12. C
13. A
14. B
15. E

16. C
17. B
18. D
19. A
20. A

21. B
22. B
23. D
24. C
25. C

SOLUTIONS TO QUESTIONS 1-9

P implies Q = original statement

Not Q implies not P = contrapositive of the original statement. A statement and its contrapositive are logically equivalent.

Q implies P = converse of the original statement

Not P implies not Q = inverse of the original statement. The converse and inverse of an original statement are logically equivalent.

P implies Q = Not P or Q.

1. The CORRECT answer is C.
   Item I is wrong because "some employees" means "at least one employee" and possibly "all employees." If it is true that all employees have fully vested pensions, then the second statement is false. Item II is correct because the second statement is the contrapositive of the first statement.

2. The CORRECT answer is D.
   Item I is wrong because the converse of a statement does not necessarily follow from the original statement. Item II is wrong because statement I implies that there are no Hutchinson family members who live outside Lindsborg.

3. The CORRECT answer is B. Item I is correct because it is composed of the same two compound statements that are simply mentioned in a different order. Item II is correct because if each person is taller than Officer Banks, then there is no person in that precinct who can possibly be shorter than Officer Banks.

4. The CORRECT answer is B.
   Item I is correct because the second statement is the contrapositive of the first statement. Item II is correct because each statement indicates that mowing the hay fields on a particular day leads to the presence of mice the next day.

5. The CORRECT answer is A.
   If Captain Rick caught his trout in the Little Pony River, then we can conclude that he was fishing there. Since statement I says that fishing in the Little Pony Rive is against the law, we conclude that Captain Rick broke the law.

6. The CORRECT answer is D.
   The number of doctors in each group, whether the same or not, has no bearing on the conclusion. There is nothing in evidence to suggest that the group of doctors sued for malpractice overlaps with the group of doctors that are pediatricians.

7. The CORRECT answer is B.
   If we are given that Kwik-E-Mart is the second store from the west, then the order of stores from west to east, is Pop-a-Shop, Kwik-E-Mart, Nightwatch, EZ-GO, and Bob's Market.

8. The CORRECT answer is B.
We are given that Stark drove at 70 miles per hour and didn't break the law. If we also know that Montana is the only state that allows a speed of 70 miles per hour, then we can conclude that Stark must have been driving in Montana or else was driving on some interstate.

9. The CORRECT answer is B.
The only additional piece of information needed is that Lynn works for Margaret. This will guarantee that Lynn receives the promised $200 bonus.

TEST 2

DIRECTIONS: Each question or incomplete statement is followed by several suggested answers or completions. Select the one that BEST answers the question or completes the statement. *PRINT THE LETTER OF THE CORRECT ANSWER IN THE SPACE AT THE RIGHT.*

Questions 1-9.

DIRECTIONS: Questions 1 through 9 measure your ability to (1) determine whether statements from witnesses say essentially the same thing and (2) determine the evidence needed to make it reasonably certain that a particular conclusion is true.
To do well on this part of the test, you do NOT have to have a working knowledge of police procedures and techniques. Nor do you have to have any more familiarity with criminals and criminal behavior than that acquired from reading newspapers, listening to radio or watching TV. To do well in this part, you must read and reason carefully.

1. Which of the following pairs of statements say essentially the same thing in two different ways?
    I. All of the teachers at Slater Middle School are intelligent, but some are irrational thinkers.
       Although some teachers at Slater Middle School are irrational thinkers, all of them are intelligent.
    II. Nobody has no friends.
        Everybody has at least one friend.
    The CORRECT answer is:
    A. I only   B. I and II   C. II only   D. Neither I nor II

    1.____

2. Which of the following pairs of statements say essentially the same thing in two different ways?
    I. Although bananas taste good to most people, they are also a healthy food.
       Bananas are a healthy food, but most people eat them because they taste good.
    II. If Dr. Jones is in, we should call at the office.
        Either Dr. Jones is in, or we should not call at the office.
    The CORRECT answer is:
    A. I only   B. I and II   C. II only   D. Neither I nor II

    2.____

3. Which of the following pairs of statements say essentially the same thing in two different ways?
    I. Some millworker work two shifts.
       If someone works only one shift, he is probably not a millworker.
    II. If a letter carrier clocks in at nine, he can finish his route by the end of the day.
        If a letter carrier does not clock in at nine, he cannot finish his route by the end of the day.
    The CORRECT answer is:
    A. I only   B. I and II   C. II only   D. Neither I nor II

    3.____

4. Which of the following pairs of statements say essentially the same thing in two different ways?
   I. If a member of the swim team attends every practice, he will compete in the next meet.
   Either a swim team member will compete in the next meet, or he did not attend every practice.
   II. All the engineers in the drafting department who wear glasses know how to use AutoCAD.
   If an engineer wears glasses, he will know how to use AutoCAD.
   The CORRECT answer is:
   A. I only   B. I and II   C. II only   D. Neither I nor II

5. Summary of Evidence Collected to Date:
   All of the parents who attend the weekly parenting seminars are high school graduates.
   Prematurely Drawn Conclusion: Some parents who attend the weekly parenting seminars have been convicted of child abuse.
   Which of the following pieces of evidence, if any, would make it reasonably certain that the conclusion drawn is true?
   A. Those convicted of child abuse are often high school graduates.
   B. Some high school graduates have been convicted of child abuse.
   C. There is no correlation between education level and the incidence of child abuse.
   D. None of the above

6. Summary of Evidence Collected to Date:
   I. Mr. Cantwell promised to vote for new school buses if he was reelected to the board.
   II. If the new school buses are approved by the school board, then Mr. Cantwell was not reelected to the board.
   Prematurely Drawn Conclusion: Approval of the new school buses was defeated in spite of Mr. Cantwell's vote.
   Which of the following pieces of evidence, if any, would make it reasonably certain that the conclusion drawn is true?
   A. Mr. Cantwell decided not to run for reelection.
   B. Mr. Cantwell was reelected to the board.
   C. Mr. Cantwell changed his mind and voted against the new buses.
   D. None of the above

7. Summary of Evidence Collected to Date:
   I. The station employs three detectives: Francis, Jackson, and Stern. One of the detectives is a lieutenant, one is a sergeant, and one is a major.
   II. Francis is not a lieutenant.
   Prematurely Drawn Conclusion: Jackson is a lieutenant.
   Which of the following pieces of evidence, if any, would make it reasonably certain that the conclusion drawn is true?
   A. Stern is not a sergeant.   B. Stern is a major.
   C. Francis is a major.   E. None of the above

8. Summary of Evidence Collected to Date:
   I. In the office building, every survival kit that contains a gas mask also contains anthrax vaccine.
   II. Some of the kits containing water purification tablets also contain anthrax vaccine.

   Prematurely Drawn Conclusion: If the survival kit near the typists' pool contains a gas mask, it does not contain water purification tablets.
   Which of the following pieces of evidence, if any, would make it reasonably certain that the conclusion drawn is true?
   A. Some survival kits contain all three items.
   B. The survival kit near the typists' pool contains anthrax vaccine.
   C. The survival kit near the typists' pool contains only two of these items.
   D. None of the above

8.____

9. Summary of Evidence Collected to Date:
   The shrink-wrap mechanism is designed to shut itself off if the heating coil temperature drops below 400 during the twin cycle.
   Prematurely Drawn Conclusion: If the machine was operating the twin cycle on Monday, it was not operating properly.
   Which of the following pieces of evidence, if any, would make it reasonably certain that the conclusion drawn is true?
   A. On Monday, the heating coil temperature reached 450.
   B. When the machine performs functions other than the twin cycle, the heating coil temperature sometimes drops below 400.
   C. The shrink-wrap mechanism did not shut itself off on Monday.
   D. None of the above

9.____

Questions 10-14.

DIRECTIONS: Questions 10 through 14 refer to Map #3 and measure your ability to orient yourself within a given section of town, neighborhood or particular area. Each of the questions describes a starting point and a destination. Assume that you are driving a car in the area shown on the map accompanying the questions. Use the map as a basis for the shortest way to get from one point to another without breaking the law.
On the map, a street marked by arrows, or by arrows and the words "One Way," indicates one-way travel and should be assumed to be one-way for the entire length, even when there are breaks or jogs in the street. EXCEPTION: A street that does not have the same name over the full length.

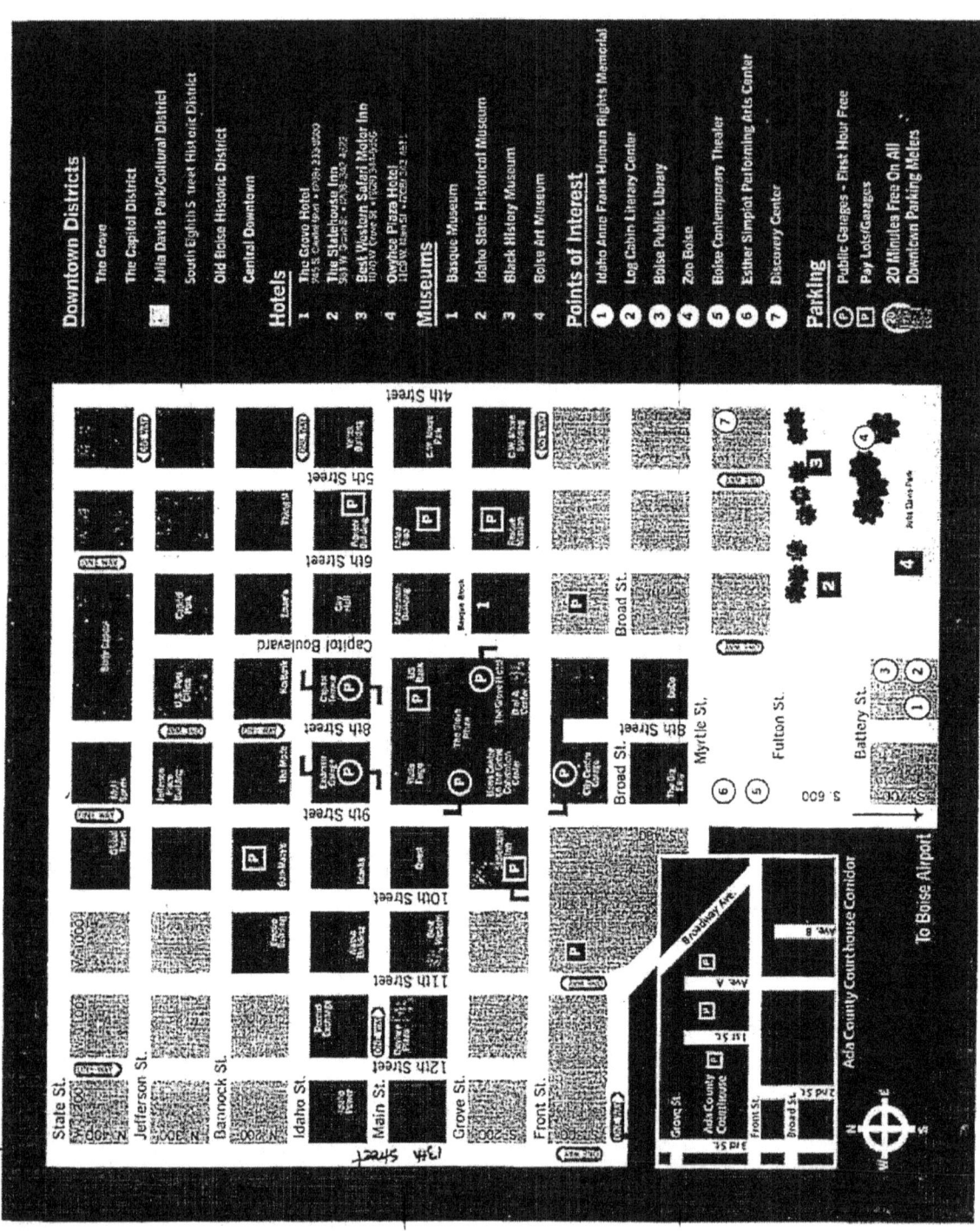

10. The SHORTEST legal way from the State Capitol to Idaho Power is
    A. south on Capitol Blvd., west on Main, north on 12th
    B. south on 8th, west on Main
    C. west on Jefferson, south on 12th
    D. south on Capitol Blvd., west on Front, north on 12th

5 (#2)

11. The SHORTEST legal way from the Jefferson Place Building to the Statesman Building is 11._____
    A. east on Jefferson, south on Capitol Blvd.
    B. south on 8th, east on Main
    C. east on Jefferson, south on 4th, west on Main
    D. south on 9th, east on Main

12. The SHORTEST legal way from Julia Davis Park to Owyhee Plaza Hotel is 12._____
    A. north on 5th, west on Front, north on 11th
    B. north on 6th, west on Main
    C. west on Battery, north on 9th, west on Front, north on Main
    D. north on 5th, west on Front, north on 13th, east on Main

13. The SHORTEST legal way from the Big Easy to City Hall is 13._____
    A. north on 9th, east on Main
    B. east on Myrtle, north on Capitol Blvd.
    C. north on 9th, east on Idaho
    D. east on Myrtle, north on 6th

14. The SHORTEST legal way from the Boise Contemporary Theater to the Pioneer Building is 14._____
    A. north on 9th, east on Main
    B. north on 9th, east on Myrtle, north on 6th
    C. east on Fulton, north on Capitol Blvd., east on Main
    D. east on Fulton, north on 6th

Questions 15-19.

DIRECTIONS: Questions 15 through 19 refer to Figure #3, on the following page, and measure your ability to understand written descriptions of events. Each question presents a description of an accident or event and asks you which of the following five drawings in Figure #3 BEST represents it.
In the drawings, the following symbols are used:
Moving vehicle ◊   Non-moving vehicle ♦
Pedestrian or bicyclist •
The path and direction of travel of a vehicle or pedestrian is indicated by a solid line.
The path and direction of travel of each vehicle or pedestrian directly involved in a collision from the point of impact is indicated by a dotted line.

In the space at the right, print the letter of the drawing that BEST fit the descriptions written below.

6 (#2)

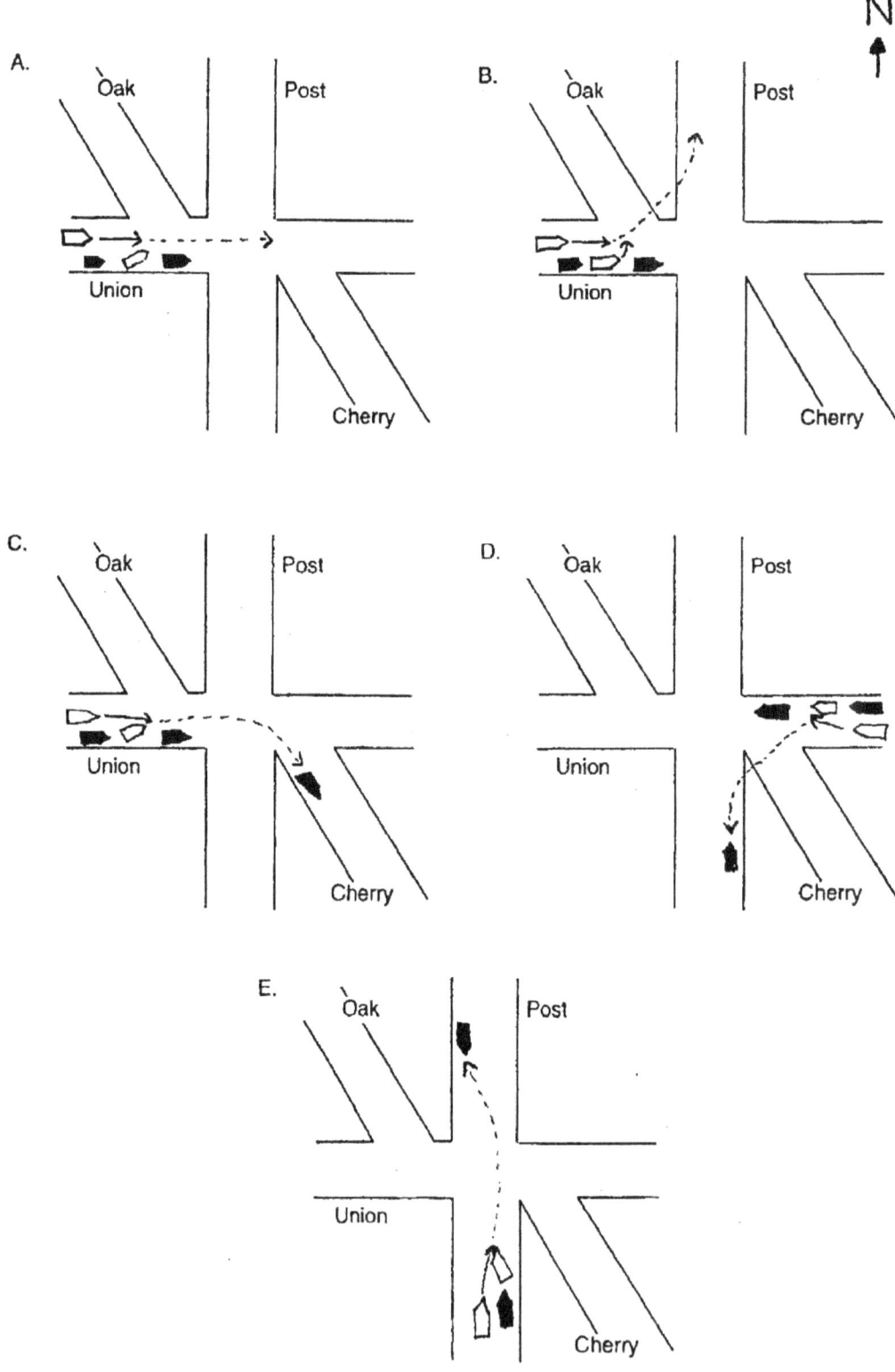

15. A driver headed east on Union strikes a car that is pulling out from between two parked cars, and then continues east. 15._____

16. A driver headed north on Post strikes a car that is pulling out from in front of a parked car, then veers into the oncoming lane and collides head-on with a car that is parked in the southbound lane of Post. 16._____

17. A driver headed east on Union strikes a car that is pulling out from two parked cars, travels through the intersection, and makes a sudden right turn onto Cherry, where he strikes a parked car in the rear. 17._____

18. A driver headed west on Union strikes a car that is pulling out from between two parked cars, and then swerves to the left. He cuts the corner and travels over the sidewalk at the intersection of Cherry and Post, and then strikes a car that is parked in the northbound lane on Post. 18._____

19. A driver headed east on Union strikes a car that is pulling out from between two parked cars, and then swerves to the left. He cuts the corner and travels over the sidewalk at the intersection of Oak and Post, and then flees north on Post. 19._____

Questions 20-22.

DIRECTIONS: In Questions 20 through 22, choose the word or phrase CLOSEST in meaning to the word or phrase printed in capital letters.

20. TITLE 20._____
 A. danger B. ownership C. description D. treatise

21. REVOKE 21._____
 A. cancel B. imagine C. solicit D. cause

22. BRIEF 22._____
 A. summary B. ruling C. plea D. motion

Questions 23-25.

DIRECTIONS: Questions 23 through 25 measure your ability to do fieldwork-related arithmetic. Each question presents a separate arithmetic problem for you to solve.

23. An investigator plans to drive from his home to Los Angeles, a trip of 2,800 miles. His car has a 24-gallon tank and gets 18 miles to the gallon. If he starts out with a full tank of gasoline, what is the FEWEST number of stops he will have to make for gasoline to complete his trip to Los Angeles? 23._____
 A. 4 B. 5 C. 6 D. 7

24. A caseworker has 24 home visits to schedule for a week. She will visit three homes on Sunday, and on every day that follows she will visit one more home than she visited on the previous day.
At the end of the day on _____, the caseworker will have completed all of her home visits.
  A. Wednesday B. Thursday C. Friday D. Saturday

25. Ms. Langhorn takes a cab from her house to the airport. The cab company charges $3.00 to start the meter and $.50 per mile after that. It's 15 miles from Ms. Langhorn's house to the airport.
How much will she have to pay for a cab?
  A. $10.50 B. $11.50 C. $14.00 D. $15.50

KEY (CORRECT ANSWERS)

1.	B		11.	D
2.	A		12.	A
3.	D		13.	B
4.	B		14.	C
5.	D		15.	A
6.	B		16.	E
7.	B		17.	C
8.	C		18.	D
9.	C		19.	B
10.	C		20.	B

21.	A
22.	A
23.	C
24.	B
25.	A

SOLUTIONS TO QUESTIONS 1-9

P implies Q = original statement

Not Q implies not P = contrapositive of the original statement. A statement and its contrapositive are logically equivalent.

Q implies P = converse of the original statement

Not P implies not Q = inverse of the original statement. The converse and inverse of an original statement are logically equivalent.

P implies Q = Not P or Q.

1. The CORRECT answer is B.
   For Item I, the irrational thinking teachers at the Middle School belong the group of all Middle School teachers. Since all teachers at the Middle School are intelligent, this includes the subset of irrational thinkers. For item II, if no one person has no friends, this implies that each person must have at least one friend.

2. The CORRECT answer is A.
   In item I, both statements state that (a) bananas are healthy and (b) bananas are eaten mainly because they taste good. In item II, the second statement is not equivalent to the first statement. An equivalent statement to the first statement would be "Either Dr. Jones is not in or we should call at the office."

3. The CORRECT answer is D.
   In item I, given that a person works one shift, we cannot draw any conclusion about whether he/she is a millworker. It is possible that a millworker works one, two, or a number more than two shifts. In item II, the second statement is the inverse of the first statement; they are not logically equivalent.

4. The CORRECT answer is B.
   In item I, any statement in the form "P implies Q" is equivalent to "Not P or Q." In this case, P = A member of the swim team attends practice, and Q = He will compete in the next meet. In item II, "P implies Q" is equivalent to "all P belongs to Q." In this case, P = Engineer wears glasses, and Q = He will know how to use AutoCAD.

5. The CORRECT answer is D. Because the number of high school graduates is so much larger than the number of convicted child abusers, none of the additional pieces of evidence make it reasonably certain that there are convicted abusers within this group of parents.

6. The CORRECT answer is B.
   Statement II is equivalent to "If Mr. Cantwell is reelected to the school board, then school buses are not approved. Statement I assures us that Mr. Cantwell will vote for new school buses. The only logical conclusion is that in spite of Mr. Cantwell's reelection to the board and subsequent vote, approval of the buses was still defeated.

10 (#2)

7. The CORRECT answer is B. From Statement II, we conclude that Francis is either a sergeant or a major. If we also know that Stern is a major, we can deduce that Francis is a sergeant. This means that the third person, Jackson, must be a lieutenant.

8. The CORRECT answer is C.
Given that a survival kit contains a gas mask, Statement I assures us that it also contains the anthrax vaccine. If the survival kit near the typist pool only contains two items, than we can conclude that the gas mask in this location cannot contain a third item, namely the anthrax vaccine.

9. The CORRECT answer is C.
The original statement can be written in "P implies Q" form, where P = the heating coil temperature drops below 400 during the twin cycle, and Q = the mechanism shuts itself off. The contrapositive (which must be true) would be "If the mechanism did not shut itself off then the heating coil temperature did not drop below 400." We would then conclude that the temperature was too high and, therefore, the machine did not operate properly.

READING COMPREHENSION
UNDERSTANDING AND INTERPRETING WRITTEN MATERIAL

EXAMINATION SECTION
TEST 1

DIRECTIONS: Each question or incomplete statement is followed by several suggested answers or completions. Select the one that BEST answers the question or completes the statement. *PRINT THE LETTER OF THE CORRECT ANSWER IN THE SPACE AT THE RIGHT.*

Questions 1-5.

DIRECTIONS: Questions 1 through 5 are to be answered on the basis of the following passage.

The laws with which criminal courts are concerned contain threats of punishment for infraction of specified rules. Consequently, the courts are organized primarily for implementation of the punitive societal reaction of crime. While the informal organization of most courts allows the judge to use discretion as to which guilty persons actually are to be punished, the threat of punishment for all guilty persons always is present. Also, in recent years a number of formal provisions for the use of non-punitive and treatment methods by the criminal courts have been made, but the threat of punishment remains, even for the recipients of the treatment and non-punitive measures. For example, it has become possible for courts to grant probation, which can be non-punitive, to some offenders, but the probationer is constantly under the threat of punishment, for, if he does not maintain the conditions of his probation, he may be imprisoned. As the treatment reaction to crime becomes more popular, the criminal courts may have as their sole function the determination of the guilt or innocence of the accused persons, leaving the problem of correcting criminals entirely to outsiders. Under such conditions, the organization of the court system, the duties and activities of court personnel, and the nature of the trial all would be decidedly different.

1. Which one of the following is the BEST description of the subject matter of the above passage?
The

   A. value of non-punitive measures for criminals
   B. effect of punishment on guilty individuals
   C. punitive functions of the criminal courts
   D. success of probation as a deterrent of crime

1._____

2. It may be INFERRED from the above passage that the present traditional organization of the criminal court system is a result of

   A. the nature of the laws with which these courts are concerned
   B. a shift from non-punitive to punitive measures for correctional purposes
   C. an informal arrangement between court personnel and the government
   D. a formal decision made by court personnel to increase efficiency

2._____

3. All persons guilty of breaking certain specified rules, according to the above passage, are subject to the threat of

   A. treatment
   B. punishment
   C. probation
   D. retrial

   3.____

4. According to the above passage, the decision whether or not to punish a guilty person is a function USUALLY performed by

   A. the jury
   B. the criminal code
   C. the judge
   D. corrections personnel

   4.____

5. According to the above passage, which one of the following is a possible effect of an increase in the *treatment reactions to crime?*

   A. A decrease in the number of court personnel
   B. An increase in the number of criminal trials
   C. Less reliance on probation as a non-punitive treatment measure
   D. A decrease in the functions of the court following determination of guilt

   5.____

Questions 6-8.

DIRECTIONS: Questions 6 through 8 are to be answered on the basis of the following passage.

A glaring exception to the usual practice of the judicial trial as a means of conflict resolution is the utilization of administrative hearings. The growing tendency to create administrative bodies with rule-making and quasi-judicial powers has shattered many standard concepts. A comprehensive examination of the legal process cannot neglect these newer patterns.

In the administrative process, the legislative, executive, and judicial functions are mixed together, and many functions, such as investigating, advocating, negotiating, testifying, rule making, and adjudicating, are carried out by the same agency. The reason for the breakdown of the separation-of-powers formula is not hard to find. It was felt by Congress, and state and municipal legislatures, that certain regulatory tasks could not be performed efficiently, rapidly, expertly, and with due concern for the public interest by the traditional branches of government. Accordingly, regulatory agencies were delegated powers to consider disputes from the earliest stage of investigation to the final stages of adjudication entirely within each agency itself, subject only to limited review in the regular courts.

6. The above passage states that the usual means for conflict resolution is through the use of

   A. judicial trial
   B. administrative hearing
   C. legislation
   D. regulatory agencies

   6.____

7. The above passage IMPLIES that the use of administrative hearing in resolving conflict is a(n) _____ approach.

   A. traditional
   B. new
   C. dangerous
   D. experimental

   7.____

8. The above passage states that the reason for the breakdown of the separation-of-powers formula in the administrative process is that

   8.____

A. Congress believed that certain regulatory tasks could be better performed by separate agencies
B. legislative and executive functions are incompatible in the same agency
C. investigative and regulatory functions are not normally reviewed by the courts
D. state and municipal legislatures are more concerned with efficiency than with legality

Questions 9-10.

DIRECTIONS: Questions 9 and 10 are to be answered SOLELY on the basis of the information given in the following paragraph.

An assumption commonly made in regard to the reliability of testimony is that when a number of persons report upon the same matter, those details upon which there is an agreement may, in general, be considered as substantiated. Experiments have shown, however, that there is a tendency for the same errors to appear in the testimony of different individuals, and that, quite apart from any collusion, agreement of testimony is no proof of dependability.

9. According to the above paragraph, it is commonly assumed that details of an event are substantiated when

   A. a number of persons report upon them
   B. a reliable person testifies to them
   C. no errors are apparent in the testimony of different individuals
   D. several witnesses are in agreement about them

10. According to the above paragraph, agreement in the testimony of different witnesses to the same event is

    A. evaluated more reliably when considered apart from collusion
    B. not the result of chance
    C. not a guarantee of the accuracy of the facts
    D. the result of a mass reaction of the witnesses

Questions 11-12.

DIRECTIONS: Questions 11 and 12 are to be answered SOLELY on the basis of the information given in the following paragraph.

The accuracy of the information about past occurrence obtainable in an interview is so low that one must take the stand that the best use to be made of the interview in this connection is a means of finding clues and avenues of access to more reliable sources of information. On the other hand, feelings and attitudes have been found to be clearly and correctly revealed in a properly conducted personal interview.

11. According to the above paragraph, information obtained in a personal interview

    A. can be corroborated by other clues and more reliable sources of information revealed at the interview
    B. can be used to develop leads to other sources of information about past events
    C. is not reliable
    D. is reliable if it relates to recent occurrences

12. According to the above paragraph, the personal interview is suitable for obtaining

   A. emotional reactions to a given situation
   B. fresh information on factors which may be forgotten
   C. revived recollection of previous events for later use as testimony
   D. specific information on material already reduced to writing

Questions 13-15.

DIRECTIONS: Questions 13 through 15 are to be answered on the basis of the following paragraph.

Admissibility of handwriting standards (samples of handwriting for the purpose of comparison) as a basis for expert testimony is frequently necessary when the authenticity of disputed documents may be at issue. Under the older rules of common law, only that writing relating to the issues in the case could be used as a basis for handwriting testimony by an expert. Today, most jurisdictions admit irrelevant writings as standards for comparison. However, their genuineness, in all instances, must be established to the satisfaction of the court. There are a number of types of documents, however, not ordinarily relevant to the issues which are seldom acceptable to the court as handwriting standards, such as bail bonds, signatures on affidavits, depositions, etc. These are usually already before the court as part of the record in a case. Exhibits written in the presence of a witness or prepared voluntarily for a law enforcement officer are readily admissible in most jurisdictions. Testimony of a witness who is considered familiar with the writing is admissible in some jurisdictions. In criminal cases, it is possible that the signature on the fingerprint card obtained in connection with the arrest of the defendant for the crime currently charged may be admitted as a handwriting standard. In order to give the defendant the fairest possible treatment, most jurisdictions do not admit the signatures on fingerprint cards pertaining to prior arrests. However, they are admitted sometimes. In such instances, the court usually requires that the signature be photographed or removed from the card and no reference be made to the origin of the signature.

13. Of the following, the types of handwriting standards MOST likely to be admitted in evidence by most jurisdictions are those

   A. appearing on depositions and bail bonds
   B. which were written in the presence of a witness or voluntarily given to a law enforcement officer
   C. identified by witnesses who claim to be familiar with the handwriting
   D. which are in conformity with the rules of common law only

14. The PRINCIPAL factor which generally determines the acceptance of handwriting standards by the courts is

   A. the relevance of the submitted documents to the issues of the case
   B. the number of witnesses who have knowledge of the submitted documents
   C. testimony that the writing has been examined by a handwriting expert
   D. acknowledgment by the court of the authenticity of the submitted documents

15. The MOST logical reason for requiring the removal of the signature of a defendant from fingerprint cards pertaining to prior arrests, before admitting the signature in court as a handwriting standard, is that

A. it simplifies the process of identification of the signature as a standard for comparison
B. the need for identifying the fingerprints is eliminated
C. mention of prior arrests may be prejudicial to the defendant
D. a handwriting expert does not need information pertaining to prior arrests in order to make his identification

Questions 16-20.

DIRECTIONS: Questions 16 through 20 are to be answered SOLELY on the basis of the information contained in the following paragraph.

A statement which is offered in an attempt to prove the truth of the matters therein stated, but which is not made by the author as a witness before the court at the particular trial in which it is so offered, is hearsay. This is so whether the statement consists of words (oral or written), of symbols used as a substitute for words, or of signs or other conduct offered as the equivalent of a statement. Subject to some well-established exceptions, hearsay is not generally acceptable as evidence, and it does not become competent evidence just because it is received by the court without objection. One basis for this rule is simply that a fact cannot be proved by showing that somebody stated it was a fact. Another basis for the rule is the fundamental principle that in a criminal prosecution the testimony of the witness shall be taken before the court, so that at the time he gives the testimony offered in evidence he will be sworn and subject to cross-examination, the scrutiny of the court, and confrontation by the accused.

16. Which of the following is hearsay?
    A(n)

    A. written statement by a person not present at the court hearing where the statement is submitted as proof of an occurrence
    B. oral statement in court by a witness of what he saw
    C. written statement of what he saw by a witness present in court
    D. re-enactment by a witness in court of what he saw

17. In a criminal case, a statement by a person not present in court is

    A. *acceptable* evidence if not objected to by the prosecutor
    B. *acceptable* evidence if not objected to by the defense lawyer
    C. *not acceptable* evidence except in certain well-settled circumstances
    D. *not acceptable* evidence under any circumstances

18. The rule on hearsay is founded on the belief that

    A. proving someone said an act occurred is not proof that the act did occur
    B. a person who has knowledge about a case should be willing to appear in court
    C. persons not present in court are likely to be unreliable witnesses
    D. permitting persons to testify without appearing in court will lead to a disrespect for law

6 (#1)

19. One reason for the general rule that a witness in a criminal case must give his testimony in court is that

    A. a witness may be influenced by threats to make untrue statements
    B. the opposite side is then permitted to question him
    C. the court provides protection for a witness against unfair questioning
    D. the adversary system is designed to prevent a miscarriage of justice

20. Of the following, the MOST appropriate title for the above passage would be

    A. WHAT IS HEARSAY?
    B. RIGHTS OF DEFENDANTS
    C. TRIAL PROCEDURES
    D. TESTIMONY OF WITNESSES

21. A person's statements are independent of who he is or what he is. Statements made by a person are not proved true or false by questioning his character or his position. A statement should stand or fall on its merits, regardless of who makes the statement. Truth is determined by evidence only. A person's character or personality should not be the determining factor in logic. Discussions should not become incidents of name calling.
According to the above, whether or not a statement is true depends on the

    A. recipient's conception of validity
    B. maker's reliability
    C. extent of support by facts
    D. degree of merit the discussion has

Question 22-25.

DIRECTIONS: Questions 22 through 25 are to be answered on the basis of the following passage.

The question, whether an act, repugnant to the Constitution, can become the law of the land, is a question deeply interesting to the United States; but, happily, not of an intricacy proportioned to its interest. It seems only necessary to recognize certain principles, supposed to have been long and well-established, to decide it. That the people have an original right to establish, for their future government, such principles as, in their opinion, shall most conduce to their own happiness, is the basis on which the whole American fabric has been erected. The exercise of this original right is a very great exertion; nor can it, nor ought it, to be frequently repeated. The principles, therefore, so established are deemed fundamental; and as the authority from which they proceed is supreme, and can seldom act, they are designed to be permanent.

22. The BEST title for the above passage would be

    A. PRINCIPLES OF THE CONSTITUTION
    B. THE ROOT OF CONSTITUTIONAL CHANGE
    C. ONLY PEOPLE CAN CHANGE THE CONSTITUTION
    D. METHODS OF CONSTITUTIONAL CHANGE

23. According to the above passage, original right is

    A. fundamental to the principle that the people may choose their own form of government
    B. established by the Constitution

C. the result of a very great exertion and should not often be repeated
D. supreme, can seldom act, and is designed to be permanent

24. Whether an act not in keeping with Constitutional principles can become law is, according to the above passage,

   A. an intricate problem requiring great thought and concentration
   B. determined by the proportionate interests of legislators
   C. determined by certain long established principles, fundamental to Constitutional Law
   D. an intricate problem, but less intricate than it would seem from the interest shown in it

25. According to the above passage, the phrase *and can seldom act* refers to the

   A. principle enacted early into law by Americans when they chose their future form of government
   B. original rights of the people as vested in the Constitution
   C. original framers of the Constitution
   D. established, fundamental principles of government

KEY (CORRECT ANSWERS)

1. C	11. B
2. A	12. A
3. B	13. B
4. C	14. D
5. D	15. C
6. A	16. A
7. B	17. C
8. A	18. A
9. D	19. B
10. C	20. A

21. C
22. B
23. A
24. D
25. A

TEST 2

DIRECTIONS: Each question or incomplete statement is followed by several suggested answers or completions. Select the one that BEST answers the question or completes the statement. *PRINT THE LETTER OF THE CORRECT ANSWER IN THE SPACE AT THE RIGHT.*

Questions 1-3.

DIRECTIONS: Questions 1 through 3 are to be answered SOLELY on the basis of the following paragraph.

    The police laboratory performs a valuable service in crime investigation by assisting in the reconstruction of criminal action and by aiding in the identification of persons and things. When studied by a technician, physical things found at crime scenes often reveal facts useful in identifying the criminal and in determining what has occurred. The nature of substances to be examined and the character of the examination to be made vary so widely that the services of a large variety of skilled scientific persons are needed in crime investigations. To employ such a complete staff and to provide them with equipment and standards needed for all possible analysis and comparisons is beyond the means and the needs of any but the largest police departments. The search of crime scenes for physical evidence also calls for the services of specialists supplied with essential equipment and assigned to each tour of duty so as to provide service at any hour.

1. If a police department employs a large staff of technicians of various types in its laboratory, it will affect crime investigations to the extent that

    A. most crimes will be speedily solved
    B. identification of criminals will be aided
    C. search of crime scenes for physical evidence will become of less importance
    D. investigation by police officers will not usually be required

1.____

2. According to the above paragraph, the MOST complete study of objects found at the scenes of crimes is

    A. always done in all large police departments
    B. based on assigning one technician to each tour of duty
    C. probably done only in large police departments
    D. probably done in police departments of communities with low crime rates

2.____

3. According to the above paragraph, a large variety of skilled technicians is useful in criminal investigations because

    A. crimes cannot be solved without their assistance as part of the police team
    B. large police departments need large staffs
    C. many different kinds of tests on various substances can be made
    D. the police cannot predict what methods may be tried by wily criminals

3.____

Questions 4-6.

DIRECTIONS: Questions 4 through 6 are to be answered SOLELY on the basis of the following passage.

Probably the most important single mechanism for bringing the resources of science and technology to bear on the problems of crime would be the establishment of a major prestigious science and technology research program within a research institute. The program would create interdisciplinary teams of mathematicians, computer scientists, electronics engineers, physicists, biologists, and other natural scientists, psychologists, sociologists, economists, and lawyers. The institute and the program must be significant enough to attract the best scientists available, and, to this end, the director of this institute must himself have a background in science and technology and have the respect of scientists. Because it would be difficult to attract such a staff into the Federal government, the institute should be established by a university, a group of universities, or an independent nonprofit organization, and should be within a major metropolitan area. The institute would have to establish close ties with neighboring criminal justice agencies that would receive the benefit of serving as experimental laboratories for such an institute. In fact, the proposal for the institute might be jointly submitted with the criminal justice agencies. The research program would require, in order to bring together the necessary *critical mass* of competent staff, an annual budget which might reach 5 million dollars, funded with at least three years of lead time to assure continuity. Such a major scientific and technological research institute should be supported by the Federal government.

4. Of the following, the MOST appropriate title for the foregoing passage is

   A. RESEARCH - AN INTERDISCIPLINARY APPROACH TO FIGHTING CRIME
   B. A CURRICULUM FOR FIGHTING CRIME
   C. THE ROLE OF THE UNIVERSITY IN THE FIGHT AGAINST CRIME
   D. GOVERNMENTAL SUPPORT OF CRIMINAL RESEARCH PROGRAMS

4._____

5. According to the above passage, in order to attract the best scientists available, the research institute should

   A. provide psychologists and sociologists to counsel individual members of interdisciplinary teams
   B. encourage close ties with neighboring criminal justice agencies
   C. be led by a person who is respected in the scientific community
   D. be directly operated and funded by the Federal government

5._____

6. The term *critical mass,* as used in the above passage, refers MAINLY to

   A. a staff which would remain for three years of continuous service to the institute
   B. staff members necessary to carry out the research program of the institute successfully
   C. the staff necessary to establish relations with criminal justice agencies which will serve as experimental laboratories for the institute
   D. a staff which would be able to assist the institute in raising adequate funds

6._____

Questions 7-9.

DIRECTIONS: Questions 7 through 9 are to be answered SOLELY on the basis of the following paragraph.

The use of modern scientific methods in the examination of physical evidence often provides information to the investigator which he could not otherwise obtain. This applies particularly to small objects and materials present in minute quantities or trace evidence because the quantities here are such that they may be overlooked without methodical searching, and often special means of detection are needed. Whenever two objects come in contact with one another, there is a transfer of material, however slight. Usually, the softer object will transfer to the harder, but the transfer may be mutual. The quantity of material transferred differs with the type of material involved and the more violent the contact the greater the degree of transference. Through scientific methods of determining physical properties and chemical composition, we can add to the facts observable by the investigator's unaided senses, and thereby increase the chances of identification.

7. According to the above paragraph, the amount of material transferred whenever two objects come in contact with one another

    A. varies directly with the softness of the objects involved
    B. varies directly with the violence of the contact of the objects
    C. is greater when two soft, rather than hard, objects come into violent contact with each other
    D. is greater when coarse-grained, rather than smooth-grained, materials are involved

8. According to the above paragraph, the PRINCIPAL reason for employing scientific methods in obtaining trace evidence is that

    A. other methods do not involve a methodical search of the crime scene
    B. scientific methods of examination frequently reveal physical evidence which did not previously exist
    C. the amount of trace evidence may be so sparse that other methods are useless
    D. trace evidence cannot be properly identified unless special means of detection are employed

9. According to the above paragraph, the one of the following statements which BEST describes the manner in which scientific methods of analyzing physical evidence assists the investigator is that such methods

    A. add additional valuable information to the investigator's own knowledge of complex and rarely occurring materials found as evidence
    B. compensate for the lack of important evidential material through the use of physical and chemical analyses
    C. make possible an analysis of evidence which goes beyond the ordinary capacity of the investigator's senses
    D. identify precisely those physical characteristics of the individual which the untrained senses of the investigator are unable to discern

Questions 10-13.

DIRECTIONS: Questions 10 through 13 are to be answered SOLELY on the basis of the information contained in the following paragraph.

Under the provisions of the Bank Protection Act of 1968, enacted July 8, 1968, each Federal banking supervisory agency, as of January 7, 1969, had to issue rules establishing minimum standards with which financial institutions under their control must comply with respect to the installation, maintenance, and operation of security devices and procedures, reasonable in cost, to discourage robberies, burglaries, and larcenies, and to assist in the identification and apprehension of persons who commit such acts. The rules set the time limits within which the affected banks and savings and loan associations must comply with the standards, and the rules require the submission of periodic reports on the steps taken. A violator of a rule under this Act is subject to a civil penalty not to exceed $100 for each day of the violation. The enforcement of these regulations rests with the responsible banking supervisory agencies.

10. The Bank Protection Act of 1968 was designed to

   A. provide Federal police protection for banks covered by the Act
   B. have organizations covered by the Act take precautions against criminals
   C. set up a system for reporting all bank robberies to the FBI
   D. insure institutions covered by the Act from financial loss due to robberies, burglaries, and larcenies

11. Under the provisions of the Bank Protection Act of 1968, each Federal banking supervisory agency was required to set up rules for financial institutions covered by the Act governing the

   A. hiring of personnel
   B. punishment of burglars
   C. taking of protective measures
   D. penalties for violations

12. Financial institutions covered by the Bank Protection Act of 1968 were required to

   A. file reports at regular intervals on what they had done to prevent theft
   B. identify and apprehend persons who commit robberies, burglaries, and larcenies
   C. draw up a code of ethics for their employees
   D. have fingerprints of their employees filed with the FBI

13. Under the provisions of the Bank Protection Act of 1968, a bank which is subject to the rules established under the Act and which violates a rule is liable to a penalty of NOT _____ than $100 for each _____.

   A. more; violation
   B. less; day of violation
   C. less; violation
   D. more; day of violation

Questions 14-17.

DIRECTIONS: Questions 14 through 17 are to be answered SOLELY on the basis of the following passage.

Specific measures for prevention of pilferage will be based on careful analysis of the conditions at each agency. The most practical and effective method to control casual pilferage is the establishment of psychological deterrents.

One of the most common means of discouraging casual pilferage is to search individuals leaving the agency at unannounced times and places. These spot searches may occasionally detect attempts at theft, but greater value is realized by bringing to the attention of individuals the fact that they may be apprehended if they do attempt the illegal removal of property.

An aggressive security education program is an effective means of convincing employees that they have much more to lose than they do to gain by engaging in acts of theft. It is important for all employees to realize that pilferage is morally wrong no matter how insignificant the value of the item which is taken. In establishing any deterrent to casual pilferage, security officers must not lose sight of the fact that most employees are honest and disapprove of thievery. Mutual respect between security personnel and other employees of the agency must be maintained if the facility is to be protected from other more dangerous forms of human hazards. Any security measure which infringes on the human rights or dignity of others will jeopardize, rather than enhance, the overall protection of the agency.

14. The $100,000 yearly inventory of an agency revealed that $50 worth of goods had been stolen; the only individuals with access to the stolen materials were the employees. Of the following measures, which would the author of the above passage MOST likely recommend to a security officer? 14._____

    A. Conduct an intensive investigation of all employees to find the culprit.
    B. Make a record of the theft, but take no investigative or disciplinary action against any employee.
    C. Place a tight security check on all future movements of personnel.
    D. Remove the remainder of the material to an area with much greater security.

15. What does the passage imply is the percentage of employees whom a security officer should expect to be honest? 15._____

    A. No employee can be expected to be honest all of the time
    B. Just 50%
    C. Less than 50%
    D. More than 50%

16. According to the above passage, the security officer would use which of the following methods to minimize theft in buildings with many exits when his staff is very small? 16._____

    A. Conduct an inventory of all material and place a guard near that which is most likely to be pilfered
    B. Inform employees of the consequences of legal prosecution for pilfering
    C. Close off the unimportant exits and have all his men concentrate on a few exits
    D. Place a guard at each exit and conduct a casual search of individuals leaving the premises

17. Of the following, the title BEST suited for this passage is 17._____

    A. CONTROL MEASURES FOR CASUAL PILFERING
    B. DETECTING THE POTENTIAL PILFERER
    C. FINANCIAL LOSSES RESULTING FROM PILFERING
    D. THE USE OF MORAL PERSUASION IN PHYSICAL SECURITY

Questions 18-24.

DIRECTIONS: Questions 18 through 24 are to be answered SOLELY on the basis of the following passage.

Burglar alarms are designed to detect intrusion automatically. Robbery alarms enable a victim of a robbery or an attack to signal for help. Such devices can be located in elevators, hallways, homes and apartments, businesses and factories, and subways, as well as on the street in high-crime areas. Alarms could deter some potential criminals from attacking targets so protected. If alarms were prevalent and not visible, then they might serve to suppress crime generally. In addition, of course, the alarms can summon the police when they are needed.

All alarms must perform three functions: sensing or initiation of the signal, transmission of the signal and annunciation of the alarm. A burglar alarm needs a sensor to detect human presence or activity in an unoccupied enclosed area like a building or a room. A robbery victim would initiate the alarm by closing a foot or wall switch, or by triggering a portable transmitter which would send the alarm signal to a remote receiver. The signal can sound locally as a loud noise to frighten away a criminal, or it can be sent silently by wire to a central agency. A centralized annunciator requires either private lines from each alarmed point, or the transmission of some information on the location of the signal.

18. A conclusion which follows LOGICALLY from the above passage is that

    A. burglar alarms employ sensor devices; robbery alarms make use of initiation devices
    B. robbery alarms signal intrusion without the help of the victim; burglar alarms require the victim to trigger a switch
    C. robbery alarms sound locally; burglar alarms are transmitted to a central agency
    D. the mechanisms for a burglar alarm and a robbery alarm are alike

19. According to the above passage, alarms can be located

    A. in a wide variety of settings
    B. only in enclosed areas
    C. at low cost in high-crime areas
    D. only in places where potential criminals will be deterred

20. According to the above passage, which of the following is ESSENTIAL if a signal is to be received in a central office?

    A. A foot or wall switch
    B. A noise-producing mechanism
    C. A portable reception device
    D. Information regarding the location of the source

21. According to the above passage, an alarm system can function WITHOUT a

    A. centralized annunciating device
    B. device to stop the alarm
    C. sensing or initiating device
    D. transmission device

22. According to the above passage, the purpose of robbery alarms is to

    A. find out automatically whether a robbery has taken place
    B. lower the crime rate in high-crime areas
    C. make a loud noise to frighten away the criminal
    D. provide a victim with the means to signal for help

23. According to the above passage, alarms might aid in lessening crime if they were 23.____

    A. answered promptly by police
    B. completely automatic
    C. easily accessible to victims
    D. hidden and widespread

24. Of the following, the BEST title for the above passage is 24.____

    A. DETECTION OF CRIME BY ALARMS
    B. LOWERING THE CRIME RATE
    C. SUPPRESSION OF CRIME
    D. THE PREVENTION OF ROBBERY

25. Although the rural crime reporting area is much less developed than that for cities and 25.____
    towns, current data are collected in sufficient volume to justify the generalization that
    rural crime rates are lower than those or urban communities.
    According to this statement,

    A. better reporting of crime occurs in rural areas than in cities
    B. there appears to be a lower proportion of crime in rural areas than in cities
    C. cities have more crime than towns
    D. crime depends on the amount of reporting

KEY (CORRECT ANSWERS)

1.	B	11.	C
2.	C	12.	A
3.	C	13.	D
4.	A	14.	B
5.	C	15.	D
6.	B	16.	B
7.	B	17.	A
8.	C	18.	A
9.	C	19.	A
10.	B	20.	D

21. A
22. D
23. D
24. A
25. B

PREPARING WRITTEN MATERIAL
EXAMINATION SECTION
TEST 1

Questions 1-15.

DIRECTIONS: For each of Questions 1 through 15, select from the options given below the MOST applicable choice, and mark your answer accordingly.
    A. The sentence is correct.
    B. The sentence contains a spelling error only.
    C. The sentence contains an English grammar error only.
    D. The sentence contains both a spelling error and an English grammar error.

1. He is a very dependible person whom we expect will be an asset to this division.   1.____

2. An investigator often finds it necessary to be very diplomatic when conducting an interview.   2.____

3. Accurate detail is especially important if court action results from an investigation.   3.____

4. The report was signed by him and I since we conducted the investigation jointly.   4.____

5. Upon receipt of the complaint, an inquiry was begun.   5.____

6. An employee has to organize his time so that he can handle his workload efficiantly.   6.____

7. It was not apparent that anyone was living at the address given by the client.   7.____

8. According to regulations, there is to be at least three attempts made to locate the client.   8.____

9. Neither the inmate nor the correction officer was willing to sign a formal statement.   9.____

10. It is our opinion that one of the persons interviewed were lying.   10.____

11. We interviewed both clients and departmental personel in the course of this investigation.   11.____

12. It is concievable that further research might produce additional evidence.   12.____

13. There are too many occurences of this nature to ignore.   13.____

135

2 (#1)

14. We cannot accede to the candidate's request.   14._____

15. The submission of overdue reports is the reason that there was a delay in   15._____
    completion of this investigation.

Questions 16-25.

DIRECTIONS: Each of Questions 16 through 25 may be classified under one of the following
              four categories:
                  A. Faulty because of incorrect grammar or sentence structure.
                  B. Faulty because of incorrect punctuation.
                  C. Faulty because of incorrect spelling.
                  D. Correct

              Examine each sentence carefully to determine under which of the above four
              options it is best classified. Then, in the space at the right, write the letter
              preceding the option which is the BEST of the four suggested above. Each
              incorrect sentence contains but one type of error. Consider a sentence to be
              correct if it contains none of the types of errors mentioned, even though there
              may be other correct ways of expressing the same thought.

16. Although the department's supply of scratch pads and stationary have   16._____
    diminished considerably, the allotment for our division has not been reduced.

17. You have not told us whom you wish to designate as your secretary.   17._____

18. Upon reading the minutes of the last meeting, the new proposal was taken   18._____
    up for consideration.

19. Before beginning the discussion, we locked the door as a precautionery   19._____
    measure.

20. The supervisor remarked, "Only those clerks, who perform routine work,   20._____
    are permitted to take a rest period."

21. Not only will this duplicating machine make accurate copies, but it will also   21._____
    produce a quantity of work equal to fifteen transcribing typists.

22. "Mr. Jones," said the supervisor, "we regret our inability to grant you an   22._____
    extention of your leave of absence.

23. Although the employees find the work monotonous and fatigueing, they   23._____
    rarely complain.

24. We completed the tabulation of the receipts on time despite the fact that   24._____
    Miss Smith our fastest operator was absent for over a week.

25. The reaction of the employees who attended the meeting, as well as the reaction of those who did not attend, indicates clearly that the schedule is satisfactory to everyone concerned.

25._____

KEY (CORRECT ANSWERS)

1.	D		11.	B
2.	A		12.	B
3.	A		13.	B
4.	C		14.	A
5.	A		15.	C
6.	B		16.	A
7.	B		17.	D
8.	C		18.	A
9.	A		19.	C
10.	C		20.	B

21. A
22. C
23. C
24. B
25. D

TEST 2

Questions 1-15.

DIRECTIONS: Questions 1 through 15 consist of two sentences. Some are correct according to ordinary formal English usage. Others are incorrect because they contain errors in English usage, spelling, or punctuation. Consider a sentence correct if it contains no errors in English usage, spelling, or punctuation, even if there may be other ways of writing the sentence correctly. Mark your answer:
    A. If only sentence I is correct.
    B. If only sentence II is correct.
    C. If sentences 1 and II are correct.
    D. If neither sentence I nor II is correct.

1. I. The influence of recruitment efficiency upon administrative standards is readily apparant.
   II. Rapid and accurate thinking are an essential quality of the police officer.

2. I. The administrator of a police department is constantly confronted by the demands of subordinates for increased personnel in their respective units.
   II. Since a chief executive must work within well-defined fiscal limits, he must weigh the relative importance of various requests.

3. I. The two men whom the police arrested for a parking violation were wanted for robbery in three states.
   II. Strong executive control from the top to the bottom of the enterprise is one of the basic principals of police administration.

4. I. When he gave testimony unfavorable to the defendant loyalty seemed to mean very little.
   II. Having run off the road while passing a car, the patrolman gave the driver a traffic ticket.

5. I. The judge ruled that the defendant's conversation with his doctor was a privileged communication.
   II. The importance of our training program is widely recognized; however, fiscal difficulties limit the program's effectiveness.

6. I. Despite an increase in patrol coverage, there were less arrests for crimes against property this year.
   II. The investigators could hardly have expected greater cooperation from the public.

7. I. Neither the patrolman nor the witness could identify the defendant as the driver of the car.
   II. Each of the officers in the class received their certificates at the completion of the course.

8. I. The new commander made it clear that those kind of procedures would no longer be permitted.
    II. Giving some weight to performance records is more advisable than making promotions solely on the basis of test scores.

9. I. A deputy sheriff must ascertain whether the debtor, has any property.
    II. A good deputy sheriff does not cause histerical excitement when he executes a process.

10. I. Having learned that he has been assigned a judgment debtor, the deputy sheriff should call upon him.
    II. The deputy sheriff may seize and remove property without requiring a bond.

11. I. If legal procedures are not observed, the resulting contract is not enforseable.
    II. If the directions from the creditor's attorney are not in writing, the deputy sheriff should request a letter of instructions from the attorney.

12. I. The deputy sheriff may confer with the defendant and enter this defendants' place of business.
    II. A deputy sheriff must ascertain from the creditor's attorney whether the debtor has any property against which he may proceede.

13. I. The sheriff has a right to do whatever is necessary for the purpose of executing the order of the court.
    II. The written order of the court gives the sheriff general authority and he is governed in his acts by a very simple principal.

14. I. Either the patrolman or his sergeant are always ready to help the public.
    II. The sergeant asked the patrolman when he would finish the report.

15. I. The injured man could not hardly talk.
    II. Every officer had ought to had in their reports on time.

Questions 16-26.

DIRECTIONS: For each of the sentences given below, numbered 16 through 25, select from the following choices the MOST correct choice and print your choice in the space at the right. Select as your answer:
A. If the statement contains an unnecessary word or expression
B. If the statement contains a slang term or expression ordinarily not acceptable in government report writing.
C. If the statement contains an old-fashioned word or expression, where a concrete, plain term would be more useful.
D. If the statement contains no major faults.

16. Every one of us should try harder.

17. Yours of the first instant has been received.

18. We will have to do a real snow job on him.   18._____
19. I shall contact him next Thursday.   19._____
20. None of us were invited to the meeting with the community.   20._____
21. We got this here job to do.   21._____
22. She could not help but see the mistake in the checkbook.   22._____
23. Don't bug the Director about the report.   23._____
24. I beg to inform you that your letter has been received.   24._____
25. This project is all screwed up.   25._____

KEY (CORRECT ANSWERS)

1.	D	11.	B
2.	C	12.	D
3.	A	13.	A
4.	D	14.	D
5.	B	15.	D
6.	B	16.	D
7.	A	17.	C
8.	D	18.	B
9.	D	19.	D
10.	C	20.	D

21. B
22. D
23. B
24. C
25. B

TEST 3

DIRECTIONS: Questions 1 through 25 are sentences taken from reports. Some are correct according to ordinary English usage. Others are incorrect because they contain errors in English usage, spelling, or punctuation. Consider a sentence correct if it contains no errors in English usage, spelling, or punctuation, even if there may be other ways of writing the sentence correctly. Mark your answer:
- A. If only sentence I is correct
- B. If only sentence II is correct
- C. If sentences I and II are correct
- D. If neither sentence I nor II is correct

1. I. The Neighborhood Police Team Commander and Team Patrolmen are encouraged to give to the public the widest possible verbal and written disemination of information regarding the existence and purposes of the program.
   II. The police must be vitally interelated with every segment of the public they serve.

2. I. If social gambling, prostitution, and other vices are to be prohibited, the law makers should provide the manpower and method for enforcement.
   II. In addition to checking on possible crime locations such as hallways, roofs yards and other similar locations, Team Patrolmen are encouraged to make known their presence to members of the community.

3. I. The Neighborhood Police Team Commander is authorized to secure, the cooperation of local publications, as well as public and private agencies, to further the goals of the program.
   II. Recruitment from social minorities is essential to effective police work among minorities and meaningful relations with them.

4. I. The Neighborhood Police Team Commander and his men have the responsibility for providing patrol service within the sector territory on a twenty-four hour basis.
   II. While the patrolman was walking his beat at midnight he noticed that the clothing stores' door was partly open.

5. I. Authority is granted to the Neighborhood Police Team to device tactics for coping with the crime in the sector.
   II. Before leaving the scene of the accident, the patrolman drew a map showing the positions of the automobiles and indicated the time of the accident as 10 M. in the morning.

6. I. The Neighborhood Police Team Commander and his men must be kept apprised of conditions effecting their sector.
   II. Clear, continuous communication with every segment of the public served based on the realization of mutual need and founded on trust and confidence is the basis for effective law enforcement.

7. I. The irony is that the police are blamed for the laws they enforce when they are doing their duty.
   II. The Neighborhood Police Team Commander is authorized to prepare and distribute literature with pertinent information telling the public whom to contact for assistance.

7.____

8. I. The day is not far distant when major parts of the entire police compliment will need extensive college training or degrees.
   II. Although driving under the influence of alcohol is a specific charge in making arrests, drunkenness is basically a health and social problem.

8.____

9. I. If a deputy sheriff finds that property he has to attach is located on a ship, he should notify his supervisor.
   II. Any contract that tends to interfere with the administration of justice is illegal.

9.____

10. I. A mandate or official order of the court to the sheriff or other officer directs it to take into possession property of the judgment debtor.
    II. Tenancies from month-to-month, week-to-week, and sometimes year-to-year are termenable.

10.____

11. I. A civil arrest is an arrest pursuant to an order issued by a court in civil litigation.
    II. In a criminal arrest, a defendant is arrested for a crime he is alleged to have committed.

11.____

12. I. Having taken a defendant into custody, there is a complete restraint of personal liberty.
    II. Actual force is unnecessary when a deputy sheriff makes an arrest.

12.____

13. I. When a husband breaches a separation agreement by failing to supply to the wife the amount of money to be paid to her periodically under the agreement, the same legal steps may be taken to enforce his compliance as in any other breach of contract.
    II. Having obtained the writ of attachment, the plaintiff is then in the advantageous position of selling the very property that has been held for him by the sheriff while he was obtaining a judgment.

13.____

14. I. Being locked in his desk, the investigator felt sure that the records would be safe.
    II. The reason why the witness changed his statement was because he had been threatened.

14.____

15. I. The investigation had just began then an important witness disappeared.
    II. The check that had been missing was located and returned to its owner, Harry Morgan, a resident of Suffolk County, New York.

15.____

16. I. A supervisor will find that the establishment of standard procedures enables his staff to work more efficiently.
    II. An investigator hadn't ought to give any recommendations in his report if he is in doubt.

17. I. Neither the investigator nor his supervisor is ready to interview the witness.
    II. Interviewing has been and always will be an important asset in investigation.

18. I. One of the investigator's reports has been forwarded to the wrong person.
    II. The investigator stated that he was not familiar with those kind of cases.

19. I. Approaching the victim of the assault, two large bruises were noticed by me.
    II. The prisoner was arrested for assault, resisting arrest, and use of a deadly weapon.

20. I. A copy of the orders, which had been prepared by the captain, was given to each patrolman.
    II. It's always necessary to inform an arrested person of his constitutional rights before asking him any questions.

21. I. To prevent further bleeding, I applied a tourniquet to the wound.
    II. John Rano a senior officer was on duty at the time of the accident.

22. I. Limiting the term "property" to tangible property, in the criminal mischief setting, accords with prior case law holding that only tangible property came within the purview of the offense of malicious mischief.
    II. Thus, a person who intentionally destroys the property of another, but under an honest belief that he has title to such property, cannot be convicted of criminal mischief under the Revised Penal Law.

23. I. Very early in it's history, New York enacted statutes from time to time punishing, either as a felony or as a misdemeanor, malicious injuries to various kinds of property: piers, boos, dams, bridges, etc.
    II. The application of the statute is necessarily restricted to trespassory takings with larcenous intent: namely with intent permanently or virtually permanently to "appropriate" property or "deprive" the owner of its use.

24. I. Since the former Penal Law did not define the instruments of forgery in a general fashion, its crime of forgery was held to be narrower than the common law offense in this respect and to embrace only those instruments explicitly specified in the substantive provisions.
    II. After entering the barn through an open door for the purpose of stealing, it was closed by the defendants.

25. I. The use of fire or explosives to destroy tangible property is proscribed by the criminal mischief provisions of the Revised Penal Law.
    II. The defendant's taking of a taxicab for the immediate purpose of affecting his escape did not constitute grand larceny.

25.____

KEY (CORRECT ANSWERS)

1. D
2. D
3. B
4. A
5. D

6. D
7. C
8. D
9. C
10. D

11. C
12. B
13. C
14. D
15. B

16. A
17. C
18. A
19. B
20. C

21. A
22. C
23. B
24. A
25. A

TEST 4

Questions 1-4.

DIRECTIONS: Each of the two sentences in Questions 1 through 4 may be correct or may contain errors in punctuation, capitalization, or grammar. Mark your answer:
- A. If there is an error only in sentence I
- B. If there is an error only in sentence II
- C. If there is an error in both sentences I and II
- D. If both sentences are correct.

1. I. It is very annoying to have a pencil sharpener, which is not in working order.
   II. Patrolman Blake checked the door of Joe's Restaurant and found that the lock has been jammed.

   1.____

2. I. When you are studying a good textbook is important.
   II. He said he would divide the money equally between you and me.

   2.____

3. I. Since he went on the city council a year ago, one of his primary concerns has been safety in the streets.
   II. After waiting in the doorway for about 15 minutes, a black sedan appeared.

   3.____

Questions 4-8.

DIRECTIONS: Each of the sentences in Questions 4 through 8 may be classified under one of the following four categories:
- A. Faulty because of incorrect grammar
- B. Faulty because of incorrect punctuation
- C. Faulty because of incorrect capitalization or incorrect spelling
- D. Correct

Examine each sentence carefully to determine under which of the above four options it is BEST classified. Then, in the space at the right, print the capitalized letter preceding the option which is the BEST of the four suggested above. Each faulty sentence contains but one type of error. Consider a sentence to be correct if it contains none of the types of errors mentioned, even though there may be other correct ways of expressing the same thought.

4. They told both he and I that the prisoner had escaped.

   4.____

5. Any superior officer, who, disregards the just complaints of his subordinates, is remiss in the performance of his duty.

   5.____

6. Only those members of the national organization who resided in the Middle west attended the conference in Chicago.

   6.____

7. We told him to give the investigation assignment to whoever was available.

   7.____

8. Please do not disappoint and embarass us by not appearing in court.

   8.____

Questions 9-13

DIRECTIONS: Each of Questions 9 through 13 consists of three sentences lettered A, B, and C. In each of these questions, one of the sentences may contain an error in grammar, sentence structure, or punctuation, or all three sentences may be correct. If one of the sentence in a question contains an error in grammar, sentence structure, or punctuation, print in the space at the right the capital letter preceding the sentence which contains the error. If all three sentences are correct, print the letter D.

9. A. Mr. Smith appears to be less competent than I in performing these duties. 9._____
    B. The supervisor spoke to the employee, who had made the error, but did not reprimand him.
    C. When he found the book lying on the table, he immediately notified the owner.

10. A. Being locked in the desk, we were certain that the papers would not be taken. 10._____
    B. It wasn't I who dictated the telegram; I believe it was Eleanor.
    C. You should interview whoever comes to the office today.

11. A. The clerk was instructed to set the machine on the table before summoning the manager. 11._____
    B. He said that he was not familiar with those kind of activities.
    C. A box of pencils, in addition to erasers and blotters, was included in the shipment of supplies.

12. A. The supervisor remarked, "Assigning an employee to the proper type of work is not always easy." 12._____
    B. The employer found that each of the applicants were qualified to perform the duties of the position.
    C. Any competent student is permitted to take this course if he obtains the consent of the instructor.

13. A. The prize was awarded to the employee whom the judges believed to be most deserving. 13._____
    B. Since the instructor believes his book is the better of the two, he is recommending it for use in the school.
    C. It was obvious to the employees that the completion of the task by the scheduled date would require their working overtime.

Questions 14-20.

DIRECTIONS: In answering Questions 14 through 20, choose the sentence which is BEST from the point of view of English usage suitable for a business report.

14. A. The client's receiving of public assistance checks at two different addresses were disclosed by the investigation.
    B. The investigation disclosed that the client was receiving public assistance checks at two different addresses.
    C. The client was found out by the investigation to be receiving public assistance checks at two different addresses.
    D. The client has been receiving public assistance checks at two different addresses, disclosed the investigation.

15. A. The investigation of complaints are usually handled by this unit, which deals with internal security problems in the department.
    B. This unit deals with internal security problems in the department usually investigating complaints.
    C. Investigating complaints is this unit's job, being that it handles internal security problems in the department.
    D. This unit deals with internal security problems in the department and usually investigates complaints.

16. A. The delay in completing this investigation was caused by difficulty in obtaining the required documents from the candidate.
    B. Because of difficulty in obtaining the required documents from the candidate is the reason that there was a delay in completing this investigation.
    C. Having had difficulty in obtaining the required documents from the candidate, there was a delay in completing this investigation.
    D. Difficulty in obtaining the required documents from the candidate had the affect of delaying the completion of this investigation.

17. A. This report, together with documents supporting our recommendation, are being submitted for your approval.
    B. Documents supporting our recommendation is being submitted with the report for your approval.
    C. This report, together with documents supporting our recommendation, is being submitted for your approval.
    D. The report and documents supporting our recommendation is being submitted for your approval.

18. A. The chairman himself, rather than his aides, has reviewed the report.
    B. The chairman himself, rather than his aides, have reviewed the report.
    C. The chairmen, not the aide, has reviewed the report.
    D. The aide, not the chairmen, have reviewed the report.

19.
   A. Various proposals were submitted but the decision is not been made.
   B. Various proposals has been submitted but the decision has not been made.
   C. Various proposals were submitted but the decision is not been made.
   D. Various proposals have been submitted but the decision has not been made.

19.____

20.
   A. Everyone were rewarded for his successful attempt.
   B. They were successful in their attempts and each of them was rewarded.
   C. Each of them are rewarded for their successful attempts.
   D. The reward for their successful attempts were made to each of them.

20.____

21. The following is a paragraph from a request for departmental recognition consisting of five numbered sentences submitted to a Captain for review. These sentences may or may not have errors in spelling, grammar, and punctuation:
(1) The officers observed the subject Mills surreptitiously remove a wallet from the woman's handbag and entered his automobile. (2) As they approached Mills, he looked in their direction and drove away. (3) The officers pursued in their car. (4) Mills executed a series of complicated manuvers to evade the pursuing officers. (5) At the corner of Broome and Elizabeth Streets, Mills stopped the car, got out, raised his hands and surrendered to the officers. Which one of the following BEST classifies the above with regard to spelling, grammar, and punctuation?
   A. 1, 2, and 3 are correct, but 4 and 5 have errors.
   B. 2, 3, and 5 are correct, but 1 and 4 have errors.
   C. 3, 4, and 5 are correct, but 1 and 2 have errors.
   D. 1, 2, 3, and 5 are correct, but 4 has errors.

21.____

22. The one of the following sentences which is grammatically PREFERABLE to the others is:
   A. Our engineers will go over your blueprints so that you may have no problems in construction.
   B. For a long time he had been arguing that we, not he, are to blame for the confusion.
   C. I worked on his automobile for two hours and still cannot find out what is wrong with it.
   D. Accustomed to all kinds of hardships, fatigue seldom bothers veteran policemen.

22.____

23. The MOST accurate of the following sentences is:
   A. The commissioner, as well as his deputy and various bureau heads, were present.
   B. A new organization of employers and employees have been formed.
   C. One or the other of these men have been selected.
   D. The number of pages in the book is enough to discourage a reader.

23.____

24. The MOST accurate of the following sentences is: 24.____
    A. Between you and me, I think he is the better man.
    B. He was believed to be me.
    C. Is it us that you wish to see?
    D. The winners are him and her.

KEY (CORRECT ANSWERS)

1.	C		11.	B
2.	A		12.	B
3.	C		13.	D
4.	A		14.	B
5.	B		15.	D
6.	C		16.	A
7.	D		17.	C
8.	C		18.	A
9.	B		19.	D
10.	A		20.	B

21. B
22. A
23. D
24. A

PREPARING WRITTEN MATERIAL

PARAGRAPH REARRANGEMENT
COMMENTARY

The sentences that follow are in scrambled order. You are to rearrange them in proper order and indicate the letter choice containing the correct answer at the space at the right.

Each group of sentences in this section is actually a paragraph presented in scrambled order. Each sentence in the group has a place in that paragraph; no sentence is to be left out. You are to read each group of sentences and decide upon the best order in which to put the sentences so as to form a well-organized paragraph.

The questions in this section measure the ability to solve a problem when all the facts relevant to its solution are not given.

More specifically, certain positions of responsibility and authority require the employee to discover connection between events sometimes, apparently, unrelated. In order to do this, the employee will find it necessary to correctly infer that unspecified events have probably occurred or are likely to occur. This ability becomes especially important when action must be taken on incomplete information.

Accordingly, these questions require competitors to choose among several suggested alternatives, each of which presents a different sequential arrangement of the events. Competitors must choose the MOST logical of the suggested sequences.

In order to do so, they may be required to draw on general knowledge to infer missing concepts or events that are essential to sequencing the given events. Competitors should be careful to infer only what is essential to the sequence. The plausibility of the wrong alternatives will always require the inclusion of unlikely events or of additional chains of events which are NOT essential to sequencing the given events.

It's very important to remember that you are looking for the best of the four possible choices, and that the best choice of all may not even be one of the answers you're given to choose from.

There is no one right way to solve these problems. Many people have found it helpful to first write out the order of the sentences, as they would have arranged them, on their scrap paper before looking at the possible answers. If their optimum answer is there, this can save them some time. If it isn't, this method can still give insight into solving the problem. Others find it most helpful to just go through each of the possible choices, contrasting each as they go along. You should use whatever method feels comfortable and works for you.

While most of these types of questions are not that difficult, we've added a higher percentage of the difficult type, just to give you more practice. Usually there are only one or two questions on this section that contain such subtle distinctions that you're unable to answer confidently. And you then may find yourself stuck deciding between two possible choices, neither of which you're sure about.

EXAMINATION SECTION

TEST 1

DIRECTIONS: Each question consists of several sentences which can be arranged in a logical sequence. For each question, select the choice which places the numbered sentences in the MOST logical sequence. *PRINT THE LETTER OF THE CORRECT ANSWER IN THE SPACE AT THE RIGHT.*

1.
   I. A body was found in the woods.
   II. A man proclaimed innocence.
   III. The owner of a gun was located.
   IV. A gun was traced.
   V. The owner of a gun was questioned.
   The CORRECT answer is:
   A. IV, III, V, II, I
   B. II, I, IV, III, V
   C. I, IV, III, V, II
   D. I, III, V, II, IV
   E. I, II, IV, III, V

   1.____

2.
   I. A man is in a hunting accident.
   II. A man fell down a flight of steps.
   III. A man lost his vision in one eye.
   IV. A man broke his leg.
   V. A man had to walk with a cane.
   The CORRECT answer is:
   A. II, IV, V, I, III
   B. IV, V, I, III, II
   C. III, I, IV, V, II
   D. I, III, V, II, IV
   E. I, III, II, IV, V

   2.____

3.
   I. A man is offered a new job.
   II. A woman is offered a new job.
   III. A man works as a waiter.
   IV. A woman works as a waitress.
   V. A woman gives notice.
   The CORRECT answer is:
   A. IV, II, V, III, I
   B. IV, II, V, I, III
   C. II, IV, V, III, I
   D. III, I, IV, II, V
   E. IV, III, II, V, I

   3.____

4.
   I. A train let the station late.
   II. A man was late for work.
   III. A man lost his job.
   IV. Many people complained because the train was late.
   V. There was a traffic jam.
   The CORRECT answer is:
   A. V, II, I, IV, III
   B. V, I, IV, II, III
   C. V, I, II, IV, III
   D. I, V, IV, II, III
   E. II, I, IV, V, III

   4.____

5. I. The burden of proof as to each issue is determined before trial and remains upon the same party throughout the trial.
    II. The jury is at liberty to believe one witness' testimony as against a number of contradictory witnesses.
    III. In a civil case, the party bearing the burden of proof is required to prove his contention by a fair preponderance of the evidence.
    IV. However, it must be noted that a fair preponderance of evidence does not necessarily mean a greater number of witnesses.
    V. The burden of proof is the burden which rests upon one of the parties to an action to persuade the trier of the facts, generally the jury, that a proposition he asserts is true.
    VI. If the evidence is equally balanced, or if it leaves the jury in such doubt as to be unable to decide the controversy either way, judgment must be given against the party upon whom the burden of proof rests.
    The CORRECT answer is:
    A. III. II, V, IV, I, VI   B. I, II, VI, V, III, IV   C. III, IV, V, I, II, VI
    D. V, I, III, VI, IV, II   E. I, V, III, VI, IV, II

5.____

6. I. If a parent is without assets and is unemployed, he cannot be convicted of the crime of non-support of a child.
    II. The term *sufficient ability* has been held to mean sufficient financial ability.
    III. It does not matter if his unemployment is by choice or unavoidable circumstances.
    IV. If he fails to take any steps at all, he may be liable to prosecution for endangering the welfare of a child.
    V. Under the penal law, a parent is responsible for the support of his minor child only if the parent is of *sufficient ability*.
    VI. An indigent parent may meet his obligation by borrowing money or by seeking aid under the provisions of the Social Welfare Law.
    The CORRECT answer is:
    A. VI, I, V, III, II, IV   B. I, III, V, II, IV, VI   C. V, II, I, III, VI, IV
    D. I, VI, IV, V, II, III   E. II, V, I, III, VI, IV

6.____

7. I. Consider, for example, the case of a rabble rouser who urges a group of twenty people to go out and break the windows of a nearby factory.
    II. Therefore, the law fills the indicated gap with the crime of *inciting to riot*.
    III. A person is considered guilty of inciting to riot when he urges ten or more persons to engage in tumultuous and violent conduct of a kind likely to create public alarm.
    IV. However, if he has not obtained the cooperation of at least four people, he cannot be charged with unlawful assembly.
    V. The charge of inciting to riot was added to the law to cover types of conduct which cannot be classified as either the crime of *riot* or the crime of *unlawful assembly*.
    VI. If he acquires the acquiescence of at least four of them, he is guilty of unlawful assembly even if the project does not materialize.
    The CORRECT answer is:
    A. III, V, I, VI, IV, II   B. V, I, IV, VI, II, III   C. III, IV, I, V, II, VI
    D. V, I, IV, VI, III, II   E. V, III, I, VI, IV, II

7.____

8. I. If, however, the rebuttal evidence presents an issue of credibility, it is for the jury to determine whether the presumption has, in fact, been destroyed.
    II. Once sufficient evidence to the contrary is introduced, the presumption disappears from the trial.
    III. The effect of a presumption is to place the burden upon the adversary to come forward with evidence to rebut the presumption.
    IV. When a presumption is overcome and ceases to exist in the case, the fact or facts which gave rise to the presumption still remain.
    V. Whether a presumption has been overcome is ordinarily a question for the court.
    VI. Such information may furnish a basis for a logical inference.
    The CORRECT answer is:
    A. IV, VI, II, V, I, III   B. III, II, V, I, IV, VI   C. V, III, VI, IV, II, I
    D. V, IV, I, II, VI, III   E. II, III, V, I, IV, VI

8.____

9. I. An executive may answer a letter by writing his reply on the face of the letter itself instead of having a return letter typed.
    II. This procedure is efficient because it saves the executive's time, the typist's time, and saves office file space.
    III. Copying machines are used in small offices as well as large offices to save time and money in making brief replies to business letters.
    IV. A copy is made on a copying machine to go into the company files, while the original is mailed back to the sender.
    The CORRECT answer is:
    A. I, II, IV, III   B. I, IV, II, III   C. III, I, IV, II   D. III, IV, II, I

9.____

10. I. Most organizations favor one of the types but always include the others to a lesser degree.
    II. However, we can detect a definite trend toward greater use of symbolic control.
    III. We suggest that our local police agencies are today primarily utilizing material control.
    IV. Control can be classified into three types: physical, material, and symbolic.
    The CORRECT answer is:
    A. IV, II, III, I   B. II, I, IV, III   C. III, IV, II, I   D. IV, I, III, II

10.____

11. I. Project residents had first claim to this use, followed by surrounding neighborhood children.
    II. By contrast, recreation space within the project's interior was found to be used more often by both groups.
    III. Studies of the use of project grounds in many cities showed grounds left open for public use were neglected and unused, both by residents and by members of the surrounding community.
    IV. Project residents had clearly laid claim to the play spaces, setting up and enforcing unwritten rules for use.
    V. Each group, by experience, found their activities easily disrupted by other groups, and their claim to the use of space for recreation difficult to enforce.

11.____

The CORRECT answer is:
A. IV, V, I, II, III
B. V, II, IV, III, I
C. I, IV, III, II, V
D. III, V, II, IV, I

12. I. They do not consider the problems correctable within the existing subsidy formula and social policy of accepting all eligible applicants regardless of social behavior.
    II. A recent survey, however, indicated that tenants believe these problems correctable by local housing authorities and management within the existing financial formula.
    III. Many of the problems and complaints concerning public housing management and design have created resentment between the tenant and the landlord.
    IV. This same survey indicated that administrators and managers do not agree with the tenants.
    The CORRECT answer is:
    A. II, I, III, IV   B. I, III, IV, II   C. III, II, IV, I   D. IV, II, I, III

12.____

13. I. In single-family residences, there is usually enough distance between tenants to prevent occupants from annoying one another.
    II. For example, a certain small percentage of tenant families has one or more members addicted to alcohol.
    III. While managers believe in the right of individuals to live as they choose, the manager becomes concerned when the pattern of living jeopardizes others' rights.
    IV. Still others turn night into day, staging lusty entertainments which carry on into the hours when most tenants are trying to sleep.
    V. In apartment buildings, however, tenants live so closely together that any misbehavior can result in unpleasant living conditions.
    VI. Other families engage in violent argument.
    The CORRECT answer is:
    A. III, II, V, IV, VI, I
    B. I, V, II, VI, IV, III
    C. II, V, IV, I, III, VI
    D. IV, II, V, VI, III, I

13.____

14. I. Congress made the commitment explicit in the Housing Act of 194, establishing as a national goal the realization of a *decent home and suitable environment for every American family*.
    II. The result has been that the goal of decent home and suitable environment is still as far distant as ever for the disadvantaged urban family.
    III. In spite of this action by Congress, federal housing programs have continued to be fragmented and grossly underfunded.
    IV. The passage of the National Housing Act signaled a few federal commitment to provide housing for the nation's citizens.
    The CORRECT answer is:
    A. I, IV, III, II   B. IV, I, III, II   C. IV, I, II, III   D. II, IV, I, III

14.____

15.
I. The greater expense does not necessarily involve *exploitation*, but it is often perceived as exploitative and unfair by those who are aware of the price differences involved, but unaware of operating costs.
II. Ghetto residents believe they are *exploited* by local merchants, and evidence substantiates some of these beliefs.
III. However, stores in low-income areas were more likely to be small independents, which could not achieve the economies available to supermarket chains and were, therefore, more likely to charge higher prices, and the customers were more likely to buy smaller-sized packages which are more expensive per unit of measure.
IV. A study conducted in one city showed that distinctly higher prices were charged for goods sold in ghetto stores in other areas.
The CORRECT answer is:
  A. IV, II, I, III   B. IV, I, III, II   C. II, IV, III, I   D. II, III, IV, I

15._____

KEY (CORRECT ANSWERS)

1.	C	6.	C	11.	D
2.	E	7.	A	12.	C
3.	B	8.	B	13.	B
4.	B	9.	C	14.	B
5.	D	10.	D	15.	C

GLOSSARY OF LEGAL TERMS

TABLE OF CONTENTS

	Page
Action ... Affiant	1
Affidavit ... At Bar	2
At Issue ... Burden of Proof	3
Business ... Commute	4
Complainant ... Conviction	5
Cooperative ... Demur (v.)	6
Demurrage ... Endorsement	7
Enjoin ... Facsimile	8
Factor ... Guilty	9
Habeas Corpus ... Incumbrance	10
Indemnify ... Laches	11
Landlord and Tenant ... Malice	12
Mandamus ... Obiter Dictum	13
Object (v.) ... Perjury	14
Perpetuity ... Proclamation	15
Proffered Evidence ... Referee	16
Referendum ... Stare Decisis	17
State ... Term	18
Testamentary ... Warrant (Warranty) (v.)	19
Warrant (n.) ... Zoning	20

GLOSSARY OF LEGAL TERMS

A

ACTION - "Action" includes a civil action and a criminal action.

A FORTIORI - A term meaning you can reason one thing from the existence of certain facts.

A POSTERIORI - From what goes after; from effect to cause.

A PRIORI - From what goes before; from cause to effect.

AB INITIO - From the beginning.

ABATE - To diminish or put an end to.

ABET - To encourage the commission of a crime.

ABEYANCE - Suspension, temporary suppression.

ABIDE - To accept the consequences of.

ABJURE - To renounce; give up.

ABRIDGE - To reduce; contract; diminish.

ABROGATE - To annul, repeal, or destroy.

ABSCOND - To hide or absent oneself to avoid legal action.

ABSTRACT - A summary.

ABUT - To border on, to touch.

ACCESS - Approach; in real property law it means the right of the owner of property to the use of the highway or road next to his land, without obstruction by intervening property owners.

ACCESSORY - In criminal law, it means the person who contributes or aids in the commission of a crime.

ACCOMMODATED PARTY - One to whom credit is extended on the strength of another person signing a commercial paper.

ACCOMMODATION PAPER - A commercial paper to which the accommodating party has put his name.

ACCOMPLICE - In criminal law, it means a person who together with the principal offender commits a crime.

ACCORD - An agreement to accept something different or less than that to which one is entitled, which extinguishes the entire obligation.

ACCOUNT - A statement of mutual demands in the nature of debt and credit between parties.

ACCRETION - The act of adding to a thing; in real property law, it means gradual accumulation of land by natural causes.

ACCRUE - To grow to; to be added to.

ACKNOWLEDGMENT - The act of going before an official authorized to take acknowledgments, and acknowledging an act as one's own.

ACQUIESCENCE - A silent appearance of consent.

ACQUIT - To legally determine the innocence of one charged with a crime.

AD INFINITUM - Indefinitely.

AD LITEM - For the suit.

AD VALOREM - According to value.

ADJECTIVE LAW - Rules of procedure.

ADJUDICATION - The judgment given in a case.

ADMIRALTY - Court having jurisdiction over maritime cases.

ADULT - Sixteen years old or over (in criminal law).

ADVANCE - In commercial law, it means to pay money or render other value before it is due.

ADVERSE - Opposed; contrary.

ADVOCATE - (v.) To speak in favor of;
(n.) One who assists, defends, or pleads for another.

AFFIANT - A person who makes and signs an affidavit.

AFFIDAVIT - A written and sworn to declaration of facts, voluntarily made.
AFFINITY- The relationship between persons through marriage with the kindred of each other; distinguished from consanguinity, which is the relationship by blood.
AFFIRM - To ratify; also when an appellate court affirms a judgment, decree, or order, it means that it is valid and right and must stand as rendered in the lower court.
AFOREMENTIONED; AFORESAID - Before or already said.
AGENT - One who represents and acts for another.
AID AND COMFORT - To help; encourage.
ALIAS - A name not one's true name.
ALIBI - A claim of not being present at a certain place at a certain time.
ALLEGE - To assert.
ALLOTMENT - A share or portion.
AMBIGUITY - Uncertainty; capable of being understood in more than one way.
AMENDMENT - Any language made or proposed as a change in some principal writing.
AMICUS CURIAE - A friend of the court; one who has an interest in a case, although not a party in the case, who volunteers advice upon matters of law to the judge. For example, a brief amicus curiae.
AMORTIZATION - To provide for a gradual extinction of (a future obligation) in advance of maturity, especially, by periodical contributions to a sinking fund which will be adequate to discharge a debt or make a replacement when it becomes necessary.
ANCILLARY - Aiding, auxiliary.
ANNOTATION - A note added by way of comment or explanation.
ANSWER - A written statement made by a defendant setting forth the grounds of his defense.
ANTE - Before.
ANTE MORTEM - Before death.
APPEAL - The removal of a case from a lower court to one of superior jurisdiction for the purpose of obtaining a review.
APPEARANCE - Coming into court as a party to a suit.
APPELLANT - The party who takes an appeal from one court or jurisdiction to another (appellate) court for review.
APPELLEE - The party against whom an appeal is taken.
APPROPRIATE - To make a thing one's own.
APPROPRIATION - Prescribing the destination of a thing; the act of the legislature designating a particular fund, to be applied to some object of government expenditure.
APPURTENANT - Belonging to; accessory or incident to.
ARBITER - One who decides a dispute; a referee.
ARBITRARY - Unreasoned; not governed by any fixed rules or standard.
ARGUENDO - By way of argument.
ARRAIGN - To call the prisoner before the court to answer to a charge.
ASSENT - A declaration of willingness to do something in compliance with a request.
ASSERT - Declare.
ASSESS - To fix the rate or amount.
ASSIGN - To transfer; to appoint; to select for a particular purpose.
ASSIGNEE - One who receives an assignment.
ASSIGNOR - One who makes an assignment.
AT BAR - Before the court.

AT ISSUE - When parties in an action come to a point where one asserts something and the other denies it.
ATTACH - Seize property by court order and sometimes arrest a person.
ATTEST - To witness a will, etc.; act of attestation.
AVERMENT - A positive statement of facts.

B

BAIL - To obtain the release of a person from legal custody by giving security and promising that he shall appear in court; to deliver (goods, etc.) in trust to a person for a special purpose.
BAILEE - One to whom personal property is delivered under a contract of bailment.
BAILMENT - Delivery of personal property to another to be held for a certain purpose and to be returned when the purpose is accomplished.
BAILOR - The party who delivers goods to another, under a contract of bailment.
BANC (OR BANK) - Bench; the place where a court sits permanently or regularly; also the assembly of all the judges of a court.
BANKRUPT - An insolvent person, technically, one declared to be bankrupt after a bankruptcy proceeding.
BAR - The legal profession.
BARRATRY - Exciting groundless judicial proceedings.
BARTER - A contract by which parties exchange goods for other goods.
BATTERY - Illegal interfering with another's person.
BEARER - In commercial law, it means the person in possession of a commercial paper which is payable to the bearer.
BENCH - The court itself or the judge.
BENEFICIARY - A person benefiting under a will, trust, or agreement.
BEST EVIDENCE RULE, THE - Except as otherwise provided by statute, no evidence other than the writing itself is admissible to prove the content of a writing. This section shall be known and may be cited as the best evidence rule.
BEQUEST - A gift of personal property under a will.
BILL - A formal written statement of complaint to a court of justice; also, a draft of an act of the legislature before it becomes a law; also, accounts for goods sold, services rendered, or work done.
BONA FIDE - In or with good faith; honestly.
BOND - An instrument by which the maker promises to pay a sum of money to another, usually providing that upon performances of a certain condition the obligation shall be void.
BOYCOTT - A plan to prevent the carrying on of a business by wrongful means.
BREACH - The breaking or violating of a law, or the failure to carry out a duty.
BRIEF - A written document, prepared by a lawyer to serve as the basis of an argument upon a case in court, usually an appellate court.
BURDEN OF PRODUCING EVIDENCE - The obligation of a party to introduce evidence sufficient to avoid a ruling against him on the issue.
BURDEN OF PROOF - The obligation of a party to establish by evidence a requisite degree of belief concerning a fact in the mind of the trier of fact or the court. The burden of proof may require a party to raise a reasonable doubt concerning the existence of nonexistence of a fact or that he establish the existence or nonexistence of a fact by a preponderance of the evidence, by clear and convincing proof, or by proof beyond a reasonable doubt.

Except as otherwise provided by law, the burden of proof requires proof by a preponderance of the evidence.

BUSINESS, A - Shall include every kind of business, profession, occupation, calling or operation of institutions, whether carried on for profit or not.

BY-LAWS - Regulations, ordinances, or rules enacted by a corporation, association, etc., for its own government.

C

CANON - A doctrine; also, a law or rule, of a church or association in particular.

CAPIAS - An order to arrest.

CAPTION - In a pleading, deposition or other paper connected with a case in court, it is the heading or introductory clause which shows the names of the parties, name of the court, number of the case on the docket or calendar, etc.

CARRIER - A person or corporation undertaking to transport persons or property.

CASE - A general term for an action, cause, suit, or controversy before a judicial body.

CAUSE - A suit, litigation or action before a court.

CAVEAT EMPTOR - Let the buyer beware. This term expresses the rule that the purchaser of an article must examine, judge, and test it for himself, being bound to discover any obvious defects or imperfections.

CERTIFICATE - A written representation that some legal formality has been complied with.

CERTIORARI - To be informed of; the name of a writ issued by a superior court directing the lower court to send up to the former the record and proceedings of a case.

CHANGE OF VENUE - To remove place of trial from one place to another.

CHARGE - An obligation or duty; a formal complaint; an instruction of the court to the jury upon a case.

CHARTER - (n.) The authority by virtue of which an organized body acts;
(v.) in mercantile law, it means to hire or lease a vehicle or vessel for transportation.

CHATTEL - An article of personal property.

CHATTEL MORTGAGE - A mortgage on personal property.

CIRCUIT - A division of the country, for the administration of justice; a geographical area served by a court.

CITATION - The act of the court by which a person is summoned or cited; also, a reference to legal authority.

CIVIL (ACTIONS)- It indicates the private rights and remedies of individuals in contrast to the word "criminal" (actions) which relates to prosecution for violation of laws.

CLAIM (n.) - Any demand held or asserted as of right.

CODICIL - An addition to a will.

CODIFY - To arrange the laws of a country into a code.

COGNIZANCE - Notice or knowledge.

COLLATERAL - By the side; accompanying; an article or thing given to secure performance of a promise.

COMITY - Courtesy; the practice by which one court follows the decision of another court on the same question.

COMMIT - To perform, as an act; to perpetrate, as a crime; to send a person to prison.

COMMON LAW - As distinguished from law created by the enactment of the legislature (called statutory law), it relates to those principles and rules of action which derive their authority solely from usages and customs of immemorial antiquity, particularly with reference to the ancient unwritten law of England. The written pronouncements of the common law are found in court decisions.

COMMUTE - Change punishment to one less severe.

COMPLAINANT - One who applies to the court for legal redress.
COMPLAINT - The pleading of a plaintiff in a civil action; or a charge that a person has committed a specified offense.
COMPROMISE - An arrangement for settling a dispute by agreement.
CONCUR - To agree, consent.
CONCURRENT - Running together, at the same time.
CONDEMNATION - Taking private property for public use on payment therefor.
CONDITION - Mode or state of being; a qualification or restriction.
CONDUCT - Active and passive behavior; both verbal and nonverbal.
CONFESSION - Voluntary statement of guilt of crime.
CONFIDENTIAL COMMUNICATION BETWEEN CLIENT AND LAWYER - Information transmitted between a client and his lawyer in the course of that relationship and in confidence by a means which, so far as the client is aware, discloses the information to no third persons other than those who are present to further the interest of the client in the consultation or those to whom disclosure is reasonably necessary for the transmission of the information or the accomplishment of the purpose for which the lawyer is consulted, and includes a legal opinion formed and the advice given by the lawyer in the course of that relationship.
CONFRONTATION - Witness testifying in presence of defendant.
CONSANGUINITY - Blood relationship.
CONSIGN - To give in charge; commit; entrust; to send or transmit goods to a merchant, factor, or agent for sale.
CONSIGNEE - One to whom a consignment is made.
CONSIGNOR - One who sends or makes a consignment.
CONSPIRACY - In criminal law, it means an agreement between two or more persons to commit an unlawful act.
CONSPIRATORS - Persons involved in a conspiracy.
CONSTITUTION - The fundamental law of a nation or state.
CONSTRUCTION OF GENDERS - The masculine gender includes the feminine and neuter.
CONSTRUCTION OF SINGULAR AND PLURAL - The singular number includes the plural; and the plural, the singular.
CONSTRUCTION OF TENSES - The present tense includes the past and future tenses; and the future, the present.
CONSTRUCTIVE - An act or condition assumed from other parts or conditions.
CONSTRUE - To ascertain the meaning of language.
CONSUMMATE - To complete.
CONTIGUOUS - Adjoining; touching; bounded by.
CONTINGENT - Possible, but not assured; dependent upon some condition.
CONTINUANCE - The adjournment or postponement of an action pending in a court.
CONTRA - Against, opposed to; contrary.
CONTRACT - An agreement between two or more persons to do or not to do a particular thing.
CONTROVERT - To dispute, deny.
CONVERSION - Dealing with the personal property of another as if it were one's own, without right.
CONVEYANCE - An instrument transferring title to land.
CONVICTION - Generally, the result of a criminal trial which ends in a judgment or sentence that the defendant is guilty as charged.

COOPERATIVE - A cooperative is a voluntary organization of persons with a common interest, formed and operated along democratic lines for the purpose of supplying services at cost to its members and other patrons, who contribute both capital and business.

CORPUS DELICTI - The body of a crime; the crime itself.

CORROBORATE - To strengthen; to add weight by additional evidence.

COUNTERCLAIM - A claim presented by a defendant in opposition to or deduction from the claim of the plaintiff.

COUNTY - Political subdivision of a state.

COVENANT - Agreement.

CREDIBLE - Worthy of belief.

CREDITOR - A person to whom a debt is owing by another person, called the "debtor."

CRIMINAL ACTION - Includes criminal proceedings.

CRIMINAL INFORMATION - Same as complaint.

CRITERION (sing.)

CRITERIA (plural) - A means or tests for judging; a standard or standards.

CROSS-EXAMINATION - Examination of a witness by a party other than the direct examiner upon a matter that is within the scope of the direct examination of the witness.

CULPABLE - Blamable.

CY-PRES - As near as (possible). The rule of *cy-pres* is a rule for the construction of instruments in equity by which the intention of the party is carried out *as near as may be*, when it would be impossible or illegal to give it literal effect.

D

DAMAGES - A monetary compensation, which may be recovered in the courts by any person who has suffered loss, or injury, whether to his person, property or rights through the unlawful act or omission or negligence of another.

DECLARANT - A person who makes a statement.

DE FACTO - In fact; actually but without legal authority.

DE JURE - Of right; legitimate; lawful.

DE MINIMIS - Very small or trifling.

DE NOVO - Anew; afresh; a second time.

DEBT - A specified sum of money owing to one person from another, including not only the obligation of the debtor to pay, but the right of the creditor to receive and enforce payment.

DECEDENT - A dead person.

DECISION - A judgment or decree pronounced by a court in determination of a case.

DECREE - An order of the court, determining the rights of all parties to a suit.

DEED - A writing containing a contract sealed and delivered; particularly to convey real property.

DEFALCATION - Misappropriation of funds.

DEFAMATION - Injuring one's reputation by false statements.

DEFAULT - The failure to fulfill a duty, observe a promise, discharge an obligation, or perform an agreement.

DEFENDANT - The person defending or denying; the party against whom relief or recovery is sought in an action or suit.

DEFRAUD - To practice fraud; to cheat or trick.

DELEGATE (v.)- To entrust to the care or management of another.

DELICTUS - A crime.

DEMUR (v.) - To dispute the sufficiency in law of the pleading of the other side.

DEMURRAGE - In maritime law, it means, the sum fixed or allowed as remuneration to the owners of a ship for the detention of their vessel beyond the number of days allowed for loading and unloading or for sailing; also used in railroad terminology.
DENIAL - A form of pleading; refusing to admit the truth of a statement, charge, etc.
DEPONENT - One who gives testimony under oath reduced to writing.
DEPOSITION - Testimony given under oath outside of court for use in court or for the purpose of obtaining information in preparation for trial of a case.
DETERIORATION - A degeneration such as from decay, corrosion or disintegration.
DETRIMENT - Any loss or harm to person or property.
DEVIATION - A turning aside.
DEVISE - A gift of real property by the last will and testament of the donor.
DICTUM (sing.)
DICTA (plural) - Any statements made by the court in an opinion concerning some rule of law not necessarily involved nor essential to the determination of the case.
DIRECT EVIDENCE - Evidence that directly proves a fact, without an inference or presumption, and which in itself if true, conclusively establishes that fact.
DIRECT EXAMINATION - The first examination of a witness upon a matter that is not within the scope of a previous examination of the witness.
DISAFFIRM - To repudiate.
DISMISS - In an action or suit, it means to dispose of the case without any further consideration or hearing.
DISSENT - To denote disagreement of one or more judges of a court with the decision passed by the majority upon a case before them.
DOCKET (n.) - A formal record, entered in brief, of the proceedings in a court.
DOCTRINE - A rule, principle, theory of law.
DOMICILE - That place where a man has his true, fixed and permanent home to which whenever he is absent he has the intention of returning.
DRAFT (n.) - A commercial paper ordering payment of money drawn by one person on another.
DRAWEE - The person who is requested to pay the money.
DRAWER - The person who draws the commercial paper and addresses it to the drawee.
DUPLICATE - A counterpart produced by the same impression as the original enlargements and miniatures, or by mechanical or electronic re-recording, or by chemical reproduction, or by other equivalent technique which accurately reproduces the original.
DURESS - Use of force to compel performance or non-performance of an act.

E

EASEMENT - A liberty, privilege, or advantage without profit, in the lands of another.
EGRESS - Act or right of going out or leaving; emergence.
EIUSDEM GENERIS - Of the same kind, class or nature. A rule used in the construction of language in a legal document.
EMBEZZLEMENT - To steal; to appropriate fraudulently to one's own use property entrusted to one's care.
EMBRACERY - Unlawful attempt to influence jurors, etc., but not by offering value.
EMINENT DOMAIN - The right of a state to take private property for public use.
ENACT - To make into a law.
ENDORSEMENT - Act of writing one's name on the back of a note, bill or similar written instrument.

ENJOIN - To require a person, by writ of injunction from a court of equity, to perform or to abstain or desist from some act.

ENTIRETY - The whole; that which the law considers as one whole, and not capable of being divided into parts.

ENTRAPMENT - Inducing one to commit a crime so as to arrest him.

ENUMERATED - Mentioned specifically; designated.

ENURE - To operate or take effect.

EQUITY - In its broadest sense, this term denotes the spirit and the habit of fairness, justness, and right dealing which regulate the conduct of men.

ERROR - A mistake of law, or the false or irregular application of law as will nullify the judicial proceedings.

ESCROW - A deed, bond or other written engagement, delivered to a third person, to be delivered by him only upon the performance or fulfillment of some condition.

ESTATE - The interest which any one has in lands, or in any other subject of property.

ESTOP - To stop, bar, or impede.

ESTOPPEL - A rule of law which prevents a man from alleging or denying a fact, because of his own previous act.

ET AL. (alii) - And others.

ET SEQ. (sequential) - And the following.

ET UX. (uxor) - And wife.

EVIDENCE - Testimony, writings, material objects, or other things presented to the senses that are offered to prove the existence or non-existence of a fact.

Means from which inferences may be drawn as a basis of proof in duly constituted judicial or fact finding tribunals, and includes testimony in the form of opinion and hearsay.

EX CONTRACTU

EX DELICTO - In law, rights and causes of action are divided into two classes, those arising *ex contractu* (from a contract) and those arising *ex delicto* (from a delict or tort).

EX OFFICIO - From office; by virtue of the office.

EX PARTE - On one side only; by or for one.

EX POST FACTO - After the fact.

EX POST FACTO LAW - A law passed after an act was done which retroactively makes such act a crime.

EX REL. (relations) - Upon relation or information.

EXCEPTION - An objection upon a matter of law to a decision made, either before or after judgment by a court.

EXECUTOR (male)

EXECUTRIX (female) - A person who has been appointed by will to execute the will.

EXECUTORY - That which is yet to be executed or performed.

EXEMPT - To release from some liability to which others are subject.

EXONERATION - The removal of a burden, charge or duty.

EXTRADITION - Surrender of a fugitive from one nation to another.

F

F.A.S.- "Free alongside ship"; delivery at dock for ship named.

F.O.B.- "Free on board"; seller will deliver to car, truck, vessel, or other conveyance by which goods are to be transported, without expense or risk of loss to the buyer or consignee.

FABRICATE - To construct; to invent a false story.

FACSIMILE - An exact or accurate copy of an original instrument.

FACTOR - A commercial agent.
FEASANCE - The doing of an act.
FELONIOUS - Criminal, malicious.
FELONY - Generally, a criminal offense that may be punished by death or imprisonment for more than one year as differentiated from a misdemeanor.
FEME SOLE - A single woman.
FIDUCIARY - A person who is invested with rights and powers to be exercised for the benefit of another person.
FIERI FACIAS - A writ of execution commanding the sheriff to levy and collect the amount of a judgment from the goods and chattels of the judgment debtor.
FINDING OF FACT - Determination from proof or judicial notice of the existence of a fact. A ruling implies a supporting finding of fact; no separate or formal finding is required unless required by a statute of this state.
FISCAL - Relating to accounts or the management of revenue.
FORECLOSURE (sale) - A sale of mortgaged property to obtain satisfaction of the mortgage out of the sale proceeds.
FORFEITURE - A penalty, a fine.
FORGERY - Fabricating or producing falsely, counterfeited.
FORTUITOUS - Accidental.
FORUM - A court of justice; a place of jurisdiction.
FRAUD - Deception; trickery.
FREEHOLDER - One who owns real property.
FUNGIBLE - Of such kind or nature that one specimen or part may be used in the place of another.

G

GARNISHEE - Person garnished.
GARNISHMENT - A legal process to reach the money or effects of a defendant, in the possession or control of a third person.
GRAND JURY - Not less than 16, not more than 23 citizens of a county sworn to inquire into crimes committed or triable in the county.
GRANT - To agree to; convey, especially real property.
GRANTEE - The person to whom a grant is made.
GRANTOR - The person by whom a grant is made.
GRATUITOUS - Given without a return, compensation or consideration.
GRAVAMEN - The grievance complained of or the substantial cause of a criminal action.
GUARANTY (n.) - A promise to answer for the payment of some debt, or the performance of some duty, in case of the failure of another person, who, in the first instance, is liable for such payment or performance.
GUARDIAN - The person, committee, or other representative authorized by law to protect the person or estate or both of an incompetent (or of a *sui juris* person having a guardian) and to act for him in matters affecting his person or property or both. An incompetent is a person under disability imposed by law.
GUILTY - Establishment of the fact that one has committed a breach of conduct; especially, a violation of law.

H

HABEAS CORPUS - You have the body; the name given to a variety of writs, having for their object to bring a party before a court or judge for decision as to whether such person is being lawfully held prisoner.
HABENDUM - In conveyancing; it is the clause in a deed conveying land which defines the extent of ownership to be held by the grantee.
HEARING - A proceeding whereby the arguments of the interested parties are heared.
HEARSAY - A type of testimony given by a witness who relates, not what he knows personally, but what others have told hi, or what he has heard said by others.
HEARSAY RULE, THE - (a) "Hearsay evidence" is evidence of a statement that was made other than by a witness while testifying at the hearing and that is offered to prove the truth of the matter stated; (b) Except as provided by law, hearsay evidence is inadmissible; (c) This section shall be known and may be cited as the hearsay rule.
HEIR - Generally, one who inherits property, real or personal.
HOLDER OF THE PRIVILEGE - (a) The client when he has no guardian or conservator; (b) A guardian or conservator of the client when the client has a guardian or conservator; (c) The personal representative of the client if the client is dead; (d) A successor, assign, trustee in dissolution, or any similar representative of a firm, association, organization, partnership, business trust, corporation, or public entity that is no longer in existence.
HUNG JURY - One so divided that they can't agree on a verdict.
HUSBAND-WIFE PRIVILEGE - An accused in a criminal proceeding has a privilege to prevent his spouse from testifying against him.
HYPOTHECATE - To pledge a thing without delivering it to the pledgee.
HYPOTHESIS - A supposition, assumption, or toehry.

I

I.E. (id est) - That is.
IB., OR IBID.(ibidem) - In the same place; used to refer to a legal reference previously cited to avoid repeating the entire citation.
ILLICIT - Prohibited; unlawful.
ILLUSORY - Deceiving by false appearance.
IMMUNITY - Exemption.
IMPEACH - To accuse, to dispute.
IMPEDIMENTS - Disabilities, or hindrances.
IMPLEAD - To sue or prosecute by due course of law.
IMPUTED - Attributed or charged to.
IN LOCO PARENTIS - In place of parent, a guardian.
IN TOTO - In the whole; completely.
INCHOATE - Imperfect; unfinished.
INCOMMUNICADO - Denial of the right of a prisoner to communicate with friends or relatives.
INCOMPETENT - One who is incapable of caring for his own affairs because he is mentally deficient or undeveloped.
INCRIMINATION - A matter will incriminate a person if it constitutes, or forms an essential part of, or, taken in connection with other matters disclosed, is a basis for a reasonable inference of such a violation of the laws of this State as to subject him to liability to punishment therefor, unless he has become for any reason permanently immune from punishment for such violation.
INCUMBRANCE - Generally a claim, lien, charge or liability attached to and binding real property.

INDEMNIFY - To secure against loss or damage; also, to make reimbursement to one for a loss already incurred by him.
INDEMNITY - An agreement to reimburse another person in case of an anticipated loss falling upon him.
INDICIA - Signs; indications.
INDICTMENT - An accusation in writing found and presented by a grand jury charging that a person has committed a crime.
INDORSE - To write a name on the back of a legal paper or document, generally, a negotiable instrument
INDUCEMENT - Cause or reason why a thing is done or that which incites the person to do the act or commit a crime; the motive for the criminal act.
INFANT - In civil cases one under 21 years of age.
INFORMATION - A formal accusation of crime made by a prosecuting attorney.
INFRA - Below, under; this word occurring by itself in a publication refers the reader to a future part of the publication.
INGRESS - The act of going into.
INJUNCTION - A writ or order by the court requiring a person, generally, to do or to refrain from doing an act.
INSOLVENT - The condition of a person who is unable to pay his debts.
INSTRUCTION - A direction given by the judge to the jury concerning the law of the case.
INTERIM - In the meantime; time intervening.
INTERLOCUTORY - Temporary, not final; something intervening between the commencement and the end of a suit which decides some point or matter, but is not a final decision of the whole controversy.
INTERROGATORIES - A series of formal written questions used in the examination of a party or a witness usually prior to a trial.
INTESTATE - A person who dies without a will.
INURE - To result, to take effect.
IPSO FACTO - By the fact iself; by the mere fact.
ISSUE (n.) The disputed point or question in a case,

J

JEOPARDY - Danger, hazard, peril.
JOINDER - Joining; uniting with another person in some legal steps or proceeding.
JOINT - United; combined.
JUDGE - Member or members or representative or representatives of a court conducting a trial or hearing at which evidence is introduced.
JUDGMENT - The official decision of a court of justice.
JUDICIAL OR JUDICIARY - Relating to or connected with the administration of justice.
JURAT - The clause written at the foot of an affidavit, stating when, where and before whom such affidavit was sworn.
JURISDICTION - The authority to hear and determine controversies between parties.
JURISPRUDENCE - The philosophy of law.
JURY - A body of persons legally selected to inquire into any matter of fact, and to render their verdict according to the evidence.

L

LACHES - The failure to diligently assert a right, which results in a refusal to allow relief.

LANDLORD AND TENANT - A phrase used to denote the legal relation existing between the owner and occupant of real estate.
LARCENY - Stealing personal property belonging to another.
LATENT - Hidden; that which does not appear on the face of a thing.
LAW - Includes constitutional, statutory, and decisional law.
LAWYER-CLIENT PRIVILEGE - (1) A "client" is a person, public officer, or corporation, association, or other organization or entity, either public or private, who is rendered professional legal services by a lawyer, or who consults a lawyer with a view to obtaining professional legal services from him; (2) A "lawyer" is a person authorized, or reasonably believed by the client to be authorized, to practice law in any state or nation; (3) A "representative of the lawyer" is one employed to assist the lawyer in the rendition of professional legal services; (4) A communication is "confidential" if not intended to be disclosed to third persons other than those to whom disclosure is in furtherance of the rendition of professional legal services to the client or those reasonably necessary for the transmission of the communication.

General rule of privilege - A client has a privilege to refuse to disclose and to prevent any other person from disclosing confidential communications made for the purpose of facilitating the rendition of professional legal services to the client, (1) between himself or his representative and his lawyer or his lawyer's representative, or (2) between his lawyer and the lawyer's representative, or (3) by him or his lawyer to a lawyer representing another in a matter of common interest, or (4) between representatives of the client or between the client and a representative of the client, or (5) between lawyers representing the client.

LEADING QUESTION - Question that suggests to the witness the answer that the examining party desires.
LEASE - A contract by which one conveys real estate for a limited time usually for a specified rent; personal property also may be leased.
LEGISLATION - The act of enacting laws.
LEGITIMATE - Lawful.
LESSEE - One to whom a lease is given.
LESSOR - One who grants a lease
LEVY - A collecting or exacting by authority.
LIABLE - Responsible; bound or obligated in law or equity.
LIBEL (v.) - To defame or injure a person's reputation by a published writing.
(n.) - The initial pleading on the part of the plaintiff in an admiralty proceeding.
LIEN - A hold or claim which one person has upon the property of another as a security for some debt or charge.
LIQUIDATED - Fixed; settled.
LIS PENDENS - A pending civil or criminal action.
LITERAL - According to the language.
LITIGANT - A party to a lawsuit.
LITATION - A judicial controversy.
LOCUS - A place.
LOCUS DELICTI - Place of the crime.
LOCUS POENITENTIAE - The abandoning or giving up of one's intention to commit some crime before it is fully completed or abandoning a conspiracy before its purpose is accomplished.

M

MALFEASANCE - To do a wrongful act.
MALICE - The doing of a wrongful act Intentionally without just cause or excuse.

MANDAMUS - The name of a writ issued by a court to enforce the performance of some public duty.
MANDATORY (adj.) Containing a command.
MARITIME - Pertaining to the sea or to commerce thereon.
MARSHALING - Arranging or disposing of in order.
MAXIM - An established principle or proposition.
MINISTERIAL - That which involves obedience to instruction, but demands no special discretion, judgment or skill.
MISAPPROPRIATE - Dealing fraudulently with property entrusted to one.
MISDEMEANOR - A crime less than a felony and punishable by a fine or imprisonment for less than one year.
MISFEASANCE - Improper performance of a lawful act.
MISREPRESENTATION - An untrue representation of facts.
MITIGATE - To make or become less severe, harsh.
MITTIMUS - A warrant of commitment to prison.
MOOT (adj.) Unsettled, undecided, not necessary to be decided.
MORTGAGE - A conveyance of property upon condition, as security for the payment of a debt or the performance of a duty, and to become void upon payment or performance according to the stipulated terms.
MORTGAGEE - A person to whom property is mortgaged.
MORTGAGOR - One who gives a mortgage.
MOTION - In legal proceedings, a "motion" is an application, either written or oral, addressed to the court by a party to an action or a suit requesting the ruling of the court on a matter of law.
MUTUALITY - Reciprocation.

N

NEGLIGENCE - The failure to exercise that degree of care which an ordinarily prudent person would exercise under like circumstances.
NEGOTIABLE (instrument) - Any instrument obligating the payment of money which is transferable from one person to another by endorsement and delivery or by delivery only.
NEGOTIATE - To transact business; to transfer a negotiable instrument; to seek agreement for the amicable disposition of a controversy or case.
NOLLE PROSEQUI - A formal entry upon the record, by the plaintiff in a civil suit or the prosecuting officer in a criminal action, by which he declares that he "will no further prosecute" the case.
NOLO CONTENDERE - The name of a plea in a criminal action, having the same effect as a plea of guilty; but not constituting a direct admission of guilt.
NOMINAL - Not real or substantial.
NOMINAL DAMAGES - Award of a trifling sum where no substantial injury is proved to have been sustained.
NONFEASANCE - Neglect of duty.
NOVATION - The substitution of a new debt or obligation for an existing one.
NUNC PRO TUNC - A phrase applied to acts allowed to be done after the time when they should be done, with a retroactive effect.("Now for then.")

O

OATH - Oath includes affirmation or declaration under penalty of perjury.
OBITER DICTUM - Opinion expressed by a court on a matter not essentially involved in a case and hence not a decision; also called dicta, if plural.

OBJECT (v.) - To oppose as improper or illegal and referring the question of its propriety or legality to the court.
OBLIGATION - A legal duty, by which a person is bound to do or not to do a certain thing.
OBLIGEE - The person to whom an obligation is owed.
OBLIGOR - The person who is to perform the obligation.
OFFER (v.) - To present for acceptance or rejection.
    (n.) - A proposal to do a thing, usually a proposal to make a contract.
OFFICIAL INFORMATION - Information within the custody or control of a department or agency of the government the disclosure of which is shown to be contrary to the public interest.
OFFSET - A deduction.
ONUS PROBANDI - Burden of proof.
OPINION - The statement by a judge of the decision reached in a case, giving the law as applied to the case and giving reasons for the judgment; also a belief or view.
OPTION - The exercise of the power of choice; also a privilege existing in one person, for which he has paid money, which gives him the right to buy or sell real or personal property at a given price within a specified time.
ORDER - A rule or regulation; every direction of a court or judge made or entered in writing but not including a judgment.
ORDINANCE - Generally, a rule established by authority; also commonly used to designate the legislative acts of a municipal corporation.
ORIGINAL - Writing or recording itself or any counterpart intended to have the same effect by a person executing or issuing it. An "original" of a photograph includes the negative or any print therefrom. If data are stored in a computer or similar device, any printout or other output readable by sight, shown to reflect the data accurately, is an "original."
OVERT - Open, manifest.

P

PANEL - A group of jurors selected to serve during a term of the court.
PARENS PATRIAE - Sovereign power of a state to protect or be a guardian over children and incompetents.
PAROL - Oral or verbal.
PAROLE - To release one in prison before the expiration of his sentence, conditionally.
PARITY - Equality in purchasing power between the farmer and other segments of the economy.
PARTITION - A legal division of real or personal property between one or more owners.
PARTNERSHIP - An association of two or more persons to carry on as co-owners a business for profit.
PATENT (adj.) - Evident.
    (n.) - A grant of some privilege, property, or authority, made by the government or sovereign of a country to one or more individuals.
PECULATION - Stealing.
PECUNIARY - Monetary.
PENULTIMATE - Next to the last.
PER CURIAM - A phrase used in the report of a decision to distinguish an opinion of the whole court from an opinion written by any one judge.
PER SE - In itself; taken alone.
PERCEIVE - To acquire knowledge through one's senses.
PEREMPTORY - Imperative; absolute.
PERJURY - To lie or state falsely under oath.

PERPETUITY - Perpetual existence; also the quality or condition of an estate limited so that it will not take effect or vest within the period fixed by law.
PERSON - Includes a natural person, firm, association, organization, partnership, business trust, corporation, or public entity.
PERSONAL PROPERTY - Includes money, goods, chattels, things in action, and evidences of debt.
PERSONALTY - Short term for personal property.
PETITION - An application in writing for an order of the court, stating the circumstances upon which it is founded and requesting any order or other relief from a court.
PLAINTIFF - A person who brings a court action.
PLEA - A pleading in a suit or action.
PLEADINGS - Formal allegations made by the parties of their respective claims and defenses, for the judgment of the court.
PLEDGE - A deposit of personal property as a security for the performance of an act.
PLEDGEE - The party to whom goods are delivered in pledge.
PLEDGOR - The party delivering goods in pledge.
PLENARY - Full; complete.
POLICE POWER - Inherent power of the state or its political subdivisions to enact laws within constitutional limits to promote the general welfare of society or the community.
POLLING THE JURY - Call the names of persons on a jury and requiring each juror to declare what his verdict is before it is legally recorded.
POST MORTEM - After death.
POWER OF ATTORNEY - A writing authorizing one to act for another.
PRECEPT - An order, warrant, or writ issued to an officer or body of officers, commanding him or them to do some act within the scope of his or their powers.
PRELIMINARY FACT - Fact upon the existence or nonexistence of which depends the admissibility or inadmissibility of evidence. The phrase "the admissibility or inadmissibility of evidence" includes the qualification or disqualification of a person to be a witness and the existence or nonexistence of a privilege.
PREPONDERANCE - Outweighing.
PRESENTMENT - A report by a grand jury on something they have investigated on their own knowledge.
PRESUMPTION - An assumption of fact resulting from a rule of law which requires such fact to be assumed from another fact or group of facts found or otherwise established in the action.
PRIMA FACUE - At first sight.
PRIMA FACIE CASE - A case where the evidence is very patent against the defendant.
PRINCIPAL - The source of authority or rights; a person primarily liable as differentiated from "principle" as a primary or basic doctrine.
PRO AND CON - For and against.
PRO RATA - Proportionally.
PROBATE - Relating to proof, especially to the proof of wills.
PROBATIVE - Tending to prove.
PROCEDURE - In law, this term generally denotes rules which are established by the Federal, State, or local Governments regarding the types of pleading and courtroom practice which must be followed by the parties involved in a criminal or civil case.
PROCLAMATION - A public notice by an official of some order, intended action, or state of facts.

PROFFERED EVIDENCE - The admissibility or inadmissibility of which is dependent upon the existence or nonexistence of a preliminary fact.

PROMISSORY (NOTE) - A promise in writing to pay a specified sum at an expressed time, or on demand, or at sight, to a named person, or to his order, or bearer.

PROOF - The establishment by evidence of a requisite degree of belief concerning a fact in the mind of the trier of fact or the court.

PROPERTY - Includes both real and personal property.

PROPRIETARY (adj.) - Relating or pertaining to ownership; usually a single owner.

PROSECUTE - To carry on an action or other judicial proceeding; to proceed against a person criminally.

PROVISO - A limitation or condition in a legal instrument.

PROXIMATE - Immediate; nearest

PUBLIC EMPLOYEE - An officer, agent, or employee of a public entity.

PUBLIC ENTITY - Includes a national, state, county, city and county, city, district, public authority, public agency, or any other political subdivision or public corporation, whether foreign or domestic.

PUBLIC OFFICIAL - Includes an official of a political dubdivision of such state or territory and of a municipality.

PUNITIVE - Relating to punishment.

Q

QUASH - To make void.

QUASI - As if; as it were.

QUID PRO QUO - Something for something; the giving of one valuable thing for another.

QUITCLAIM (v.) - To release or relinquish claim or title to, especially in deeds to realty.

QUO WARRANTO - A legal procedure to test an official's right to a public office or the right to hold a franchise, or to hold an office in a domestic corporation.

R

RATIFY - To approve and sanction.

REAL PROPERTY - Includes lands, tenements, and hereditaments.

REALTY - A brief term for real property.

REBUT - To contradict; to refute, especially by evidence and arguments.

RECEIVER - A person who is appointed by the court to receive, and hold in trust property in litigation.

RECIDIVIST - Habitual criminal.

RECIPROCAL - Mutual.

RECOUPMENT - To keep back or get something which is due; also, it is the right of a defendant to have a deduction from the amount of the plaintiff's damages because the plaintiff has not fulfilled his part of the same contract.

RECROSS EXAMINATION - Examination of a witness by a cross-examiner subsequent to a redirect examination of the witness.

REDEEM - To release an estate or article from mortgage or pledge by paying the debt for which it stood as security.

REDIRECT EXAMINATION - Examination of a witness by the direct examiner subsequent to the cross-examination of the witness.

REFEREE - A person to whom a cause pending in a court is referred by the court, to take testimony, hear the parties, and report thereon to the court.

REFERENDUM - A method of submitting an important legislative or administrative matter to a direct vote of the people.
RELEVANT EVIDENCE - Evidence including evidence relevant to the credulity of a witness or hearsay declarant, having any tendency in reason to prove or disprove any disputed fact that is of consequence to the determination of the action.
REMAND - To send a case back to the lower court from which it came, for further proceedings.
REPLEVIN - An action to recover goods or chattels wrongfully taken or detained.
REPLY (REPLICATION) - Generally, a reply is what the plaintiff or other person who has instituted proceedings says in answer to the defendant's case.
RE JUDICATA - A thing judicially acted upon or decided.
RES ADJUDICATA - Doctrine that an issue or dispute litigated and determined in a case between the opposing parties is deemed permanently decided between these parties.
RESCIND (RECISSION) - To avoid or cancel a contract.
RESPONDENT - A defendant in a proceeding in chancery or admiralty; also, the person who contends against the appeal in a case.
RESTITUTION - In equity, it is the restoration of both parties to their original condition (when practicable), upon the rescission of a contract for fraud or similar cause.
RETROACTIVE (RETROSPECTIVE) - Looking back; effective as of a prior time.
REVERSED - A term used by appellate courts to indicate that the decision of the lower court in the case before it has been set aside.
REVOKE - To recall or cancel.
RIPARIAN (RIGHTS) - The rights of a person owning land containing or bordering on a water course or other body of water, such as lakes and rivers.

S

SALE - A contract whereby the ownership of property is transferred from one person to another for a sum of money or for any consideration.
SANCTION - A penalty or punishment provided as a means of enforcing obedience to a law; also, an authorization.
SATISFACTION - The discharge of an obligation by paying a party what is due to him; or what is awarded to him by the judgment of a court or otherwise.
SCIENTER - Knowingly; also, it is used in pleading to denote the defendant's guilty knowledge.
SCINTILLA - A spark; also the least particle.
SECRET OF STATE - Governmental secret relating to the national defense or the international relations of the United States.
SECURITY - Indemnification; the term is applied to an obligation, such as a mortgage or deed of trust, given by a debtor to insure the payment or performance of his debt, by furnishing the creditor with a resource to be used in case of the debtor's failure to fulfill the principal obligation.
SENTENCE - The judgment formally pronounced by the court or judge upon the defendant after his conviction in a criminal prosecution.
SET-OFF - A claim or demand which one party in an action credits against the claim of the opposing party.
SHALL and MAY - "Shall" is mandatory and "may" is permissive.
SITUS - Location.
SOVEREIGN - A person, body or state in which independent and supreme authority is vested.
STARE DECISIS - To follow decided cases.

STATE - "State" means this State, unless applied to the different parts of the United States. In the latter case, it includes any state, district, commonwealth, territory or insular possession of the United States, including the District of Columbia.

STATEMENT - (a) Oral or written verbal expression or (b) nonverbal conduct of a person intended by him as a substitute for oral or written verbal expression.

STATUTE - An act of the legislature. Includes a treaty.

STATUTE OF LIMITATION - A statute limiting the time to bring an action after the right of action has arisen.

STAY - To hold in abeyance an order of a court.

STIPULATION - Any agreement made by opposing attorneys regulating any matter incidental to the proceedings or trial.

SUBORDINATION (AGREEMENT) - An agreement making one's rights inferior to or of a lower rank than another's.

SUBORNATION - The crime of procuring a person to lie or to make false statements to a court.

SUBPOENA - A writ or order directed to a person, and requiring his attendance at a particular time and place to testify as a witness.

SUBPOENA DUCES TECUM - A subpoena used, not only for the purpose of compelling witnesses to attend in court, but also requiring them to bring with them books or documents which may be in their possession, and which may tend to elucidate the subject matter of the trial.

SUBROGATION - The substituting of one for another as a creditor, the new creditor succeeding to the former's rights.

SUBSIDY - A government grant to assist a private enterprise deemed advantageous to the public.

SUI GENERIS - Of the same kind.

SUIT - Any civil proceeding by a person or persons against another or others in a court of justice by which the plaintiff pursues the remedies afforded him by law.

SUMMONS - A notice to a defendant that an action against him has been commenced and requiring him to appear in court and answer the complaint.

SUPRA - Above; this word occurring by itself in a book refers the reader to a previous part of the book.

SURETY - A person who binds himself for the payment of a sum of money, or for the performance of something else, for another.

SURPLUSAGE - Extraneous or unnecessary matter.

SURVIVORSHIP - A term used when a person becomes entitled to property by reason of his having survived another person who had an interest in the property.

SUSPEND SENTENCE - Hold back a sentence pending good behavior of prisoner.

SYLLABUS - A note prefixed to a report, especially a case, giving a brief statement of the court's ruling on different issues of the case.

T

TALESMAN - Person summoned to fill a panel of jurors.

TENANT - One who holds or possesses lands by any kind of right or title; also, one who has the temporary use and occupation of real property owned by another person (landlord), the duration and terms of his tenancy being usually fixed by an instrument called "a lease."

TENDER - An offer of money; an expression of willingness to perform a contract according to its terms.

TERM - When used with reference to a court, it signifies the period of time during which the court holds a session, usually of several weeks or months duration.

TESTAMENTARY - Pertaining to a will or the administration of a will.
TESTATOR (male)
TESTATRIX (female) - One who makes or has made a testament or will.
TESTIFY (TESTIMONY) - To give evidence under oath as a witness.
TO WIT - That is to say; namely.
TORT - Wrong; injury to the person.
TRANSITORY - Passing from place to place.
TRESPASS - Entry into another's ground, illegally.
TRIAL - The examination of a cause, civil or criminal, before a judge who has jurisdiction over it, according to the laws of the land.
TRIER OF FACT - Includes (a) the jury and (b) the court when the court is trying an issue of fact other than one relating to the admissibility of evidence.
TRUST - A right of property, real or personal, held by one party for the benefit of another.
TRUSTEE - One who lawfully holds property in custody for the benefit of another.

U

UNAVAILABLE AS A WITNESS - The declarant is (1) Exempted or precluded on the ground of privilege from testifying concerning the matter to which his statement is relevant; (2) Disqualified from testifying to the matter; (3) Dead or unable to attend or to testify at the hearing because of then existing physical or mental illness or infirmity; (4) Absent from the hearing and the court is unable to compel his attendance by its process; or (5) Absent from the hearing and the proponent of his statement has exercised reasonable diligence but has been unable to procure his attendance by the court's process.
ULTRA VIRES - Acts beyond the scope and power of a corporation, association, etc.
UNILATERAL - One-sided; obligation upon, or act of one party.
USURY - Unlawful interest on a loan.

V

VACATE - To set aside; to move out.
VARIANCE - A discrepancy or disagreement between two instruments or two aspects of the same case, which by law should be consistent.
VENDEE - A purchaser or buyer.
VENDOR - The person who transfers property by sale, particularly real estate; the term "seller" is used more commonly for one who sells personal property.
VENIREMEN - Persons ordered to appear to serve on a jury or composing a panel of jurors.
VENUE - The place at which an action is tried, generally based on locality or judicial district in which an injury occurred or a material fact happened.
VERDICT - The formal decision or finding of a jury.
VERIFY - To confirm or substantiate by oath.
VEST - To accrue to.
VOID - Having no legal force or binding effect.
VOIR DIRE - Preliminary examination of a witness or a juror to test competence, interest, prejudice, etc.

W

WAIVE - To give up a right.
WAIVER - The intentional or voluntary relinquishment of a known right.
WARRANT (WARRANTY) (v.) - To promise that a certain fact or state of facts, in relation to the subject matter, is, or shall be, as it is represented to be.

WARRANT (n.) - A writ issued by a judge, or other competent authority, addressed to a sheriff, or other officer, requiring him to arrest the person therein named, and bring him before the judge or court to answer or be examined regarding the offense with which he is charged.

WRIT - An order or process issued in the name of the sovereign or in the name of a court or judicial officer, commanding the performance or nonperformance of some act.

WRITING - Handwriting, typewriting, printing, photostating, photographing and every other means of recording upon any tangible thing any form of communication or representation, including letters, words, pictures, sounds, or symbols, or combinations thereof.

WRITINGS AND RECORDINGS - Consists of letters, words, or numbers, or their equivalent, set down by handwriting, typewriting, printing, photostating, photographing, magnetic impulse, mechanical or electronic recording, or other form of data compilation.

Y

YEA AND NAY - Yes and no.

YELLOW DOG CONTRACT - A contract by which employer requires employee to sign an instrument promising as condition that he will not join a union during its continuance, and will be discharged if he does join.

Z

ZONING - The division of a city by legislative regulation into districts and the prescription and application in each district of regulations having to do with structural and architectural designs of buildings and of regulations prescribing use to which buildings within designated districts may be put.

www.ingramcontent.com/pod-product-compliance
Lightning Source LLC
Chambersburg PA
CBHW082040300426
44117CB00015B/2555